DISPLA

Ashamed

Laura Walsh suffered from a twenty-year addiction to painkillers and alcohol before rebuilding her life to become the director of a highly successful company. When not overseeing her business, she spends time with her son, daughter and three granddaughters.

Ashamed

LAURA WALSH

MAINSTREAM
PUBLISHING

EDINBURGH AND LONDON

First published in Great Britain in 2011 by
MAINSTREAM PUBLISHING COMPANY
(EDINBURGH) LTD
7 Albany Street
Edinburgh EH1 3UG

ISBN 9781845967635

A catalogue record for this book is available
from the British Library

Typeset in Giovanni

Printed in Great Britain by
CPI Cox & Wyman Reading RG1 8EX

1 3 5 7 9 10 8 6 4 2

To Karissa, Ricky and Natasha.

Karissa and Ricky, you were my strength when I was weak,
held me up when I fell down and saw the
good in me that no one else could.
For this I am eternally grateful.

Natasha – my angel whom I loved with all my heart.
I will forever cherish the memories of you, Natasha.
You will always have a special place in my heart.

Acknowledgements

Kerry Waldron – 'my rock', *always* there for me! I love you, 'twin sister'.

Nathan Parry – who loves me unconditionally and in a way no other man has loved me before.

Annette Butler – to whom I will forever be in debt for her selfless actions on that fateful day. You are my best friend.

Kevin Walsh – brother, I believe you saved my life. I owe you so much more than words can say.

Dawn Bruno – you put up with so much from me over the years, but you never stopped loving me. Thank you!

Maureen Walsh – Mum, we have had our ups and downs, been through thick and thin. You are the mother who gave me more than I realise.

Shaun Walsh – my eldest brother, thank you for being 'the man of the house' when Dad was not there.

David Wilson – for putting my jumbled thoughts into words and making the impossible possible, thank you.

Frank Walsh – Dad, thank you for being my dad. No other man would have been good enough.

Isabel Atherton – my agent. Thank you for all your hard work.

Simone Butler – the inspiration behind me writing this book.

Andy and Sonia Morris – the best auntie and uncle. Thank you for being there for me and my family in our time of need.

Coniston Medical Practice – for referring me to Blackberry Hill Hospital and never judging me, and more importantly for not 'striking me off'.

Mainstream Publishing – thank you for believing in me and giving me the opportunity to tell my life story.

Pat Hedges – thank you for being an amazing godmother.

Raj – thank you for your support.

There are so many other people who deserve my gratitude, but I cannot name them all here. I hope they know who they are. Thank you all.

Contents

Preface

Hope. Six years ago, I finally understood the power of that emotion. It is the reason I wanted to write this book. I haven't found it an easy task, but when the tears flowed or the shame flushed my cheeks, that word pushed me to the end. Hope.

I have tried to tell my story as honestly as I can, attempting to provide a doorway into the world in which I lived, where the reader can breathe the same air, perhaps at times feeling disgust and anger at the way I used that oxygen to conduct my life. It is for others to assess whether I have achieved my aim, but this is a genuine account of a life from which I found it impossible to escape for many years, even though I was desperate to do so. My addictions proved so strong that time and time again they pulled me back when I thought I had broken free, and in the end they almost killed me.

There would be no point in telling my story with anything less than complete candour. This is how I remember the key moments that shaped my life. Others who were there may have seen the events differently. They are not wrong. Neither am I. In writing this, what I have come to realise is that every life story can be interpreted in many ways, all of them truthful. This is my truth.

That said, and in the spirit of honesty, for legal or other personal reasons I have changed some names and details and omitted certain events. To have done otherwise would only have resulted in hurt to others. Nothing that has been altered distorts the essence of what happened.

Ashamed

I hope this book gives something back for the time you invest in reading it, be it the comfort of knowing that none of us are alone in facing dark days or merely the experience of joining me on the roller-coaster ride that was my life. If you close this book with the satisfaction of having been told an interesting tale and with an ounce more strength to take a positive step forward, I will be thrilled and honoured.

Thank you. I wish you peace and hope for the future.

Laura Walsh, 2011

Introduction

May 2010

You look a mess, Laura Walsh.

I am staring at myself in the mirror. Bandages cover the right side of my face. I can see bruising creeping under my left eye and there's swelling around my nose. Not surprising. I've just had emergency surgery. I am determined to make it the last I ever have on my face. This is it.

Two weeks ago, I received the prints from a photo shoot I had arranged. The pictures were stunning. I couldn't have been happier. After undergoing countless operations to undo the hurt I had inflicted on myself, to recapture the youth that the poisons I had willingly put into my body had stolen from me, I was finally happy with my appearance. It was my last step in banishing the old Laura for ever. For years, I had had a vision of how I should look, and at last I had realised my dream. It had cost me thousands of pounds, money I had worked hard to earn after years in the wilderness, but it had been worth it. It was a final new beginning for Laura Walsh, after so many false dawns. Until the pain in my cheek warned me something was seriously wrong.

Within hours of that first discomfort, the swelling was visible. By the following day, my eye was swollen shut and the side of my face was three times the size it should have been, the skin tight, red, nasty. In less than 24 hours, my hopes were being stripped away. I had endured so much to arrive at this point. It was too much to bear.

'Your cheek implant must be infected,' the surgeon told

13

me. No shit. I had been in and out of enough hospitals to know that. Three rounds of antibiotics provided no relief. Then the words I had been dreading: 'I am going to have to operate. I have never seen anything quite like this before. It has to be cleaned out as soon as possible. Today, if you can make it.'

Oh, I could make it. If I had to endure this final procedure, then I would. Fix the problem and I will be content. Give me back my perfect face.

That was only yesterday, the operation last night. Now, here I am, in my bathroom at home. I have to see. I can't remember anything from when I came round. Did they say it had gone well? I was too out of it to understand. A taxi home to a restless sleep, waking to a moment of revelation.

The surgical tape is stuck firm, but after a moment my fingers loosen a corner. Tug gently, Laura. Don't hurt yourself. But I am impatient. I am always impatient. I want everything now, right now.

I begin to peel back the tape. It is catching on the surgical wadding packed in there. Why is there so much? Carefully, I tease it away. I lean in closer to the mirror. Dried blood? I am going to have to tug the dressing off. I've faced a lot worse. Here goes.

The streaks of blood obscure the reflection staring back at me. For a moment, I think my vision is blurred, before another spurt of crimson splashes down into the sink, making obscene patterns as it hits the porcelain. It is pissing out of me. Blood is pouring down my face.

No! No, no, no, no, no. No!

Did I faint? I don't think so. I am still here at the mirror. What happened? I can't bear to look up. I can't raise my eyes. I don't want to see my face again.

But I look. Of course I do.

When I wipe away the blood from the mirror, I see a gaping, raw, ragged hole where my cheek should be. The bone and tissue are visible. It is as though someone has put a shotgun to my face and pulled the trigger. The white walls and ceiling of the bathroom come rushing towards me. I feel sick. I can barely stand.

Am I being punished? Have I deserved this? I have let so many people down in my life. My family. My poor baby girl. Myself. This must be payback.

How did I get here? What happened to the little girl who wished only for happiness, for children and to be somebody?

Chapter One
Don't Leave Me, Please

Christmas Eve 1970

I know Father Christmas has been because I can feel the weight of the stocking he has left for me at the foot of my bed.

I am always amazed that I never wake up when he comes down the chimney. He must make a lot of noise. We only have a small fire at home and Father Christmas is big and fat. I know because I have seen loads of pictures of him. But I never hear anything. It's magic, I suppose.

I look down at my little sister, Dawn, lying on her tiny bed in the bunk below. She is still asleep. Good, I think. I can open my presents in peace. I slip out of bed, careful not to disturb Dawn. It is freezing cold, so I put on my slippers and the dressing gown that Mum made for me, and I sit on the floor. Father Christmas's stocking is at my feet. There is just enough light for me to see my presents bulging out of a sort of nylon sack. It looks a lot like the tights Mum wears.

Silently, I pull out my presents, one at a time: a colouring book, pencils, new socks, a hat, plasticine, two apples and an orange. Lots of things I want. Father Christmas knows I have been a good girl all year. Daddy's special girl, that's me. Or it was until Dawn came along and ruined everything.

She is still asleep, her stocking full and untouched. She still has all that fun to look forward to. Then I have a thought. No one will know if I take one. Father Christmas won't mind. He knows it isn't fair that Dawn is here. He knows I deserve one more.

I reach across and carefully lift out the biggest present, which is poking out of the top, and quickly unwrap it. A Fuzzy-Felt farm. Dawn is not even four and I am almost six and a half. She will just lose all the animals. It must have been meant for me.

Later, when Mum sees me playing with it, she makes me give it back. I don't understand how she knows it belongs to Dawn. Magic again. But to me it is another example of how Dawn has spoiled everything.

By the time I could walk, I knew I was special. Dad always said so. I had two brothers, Shaun, who is four years older than me, and Kevin, three years older. Even at three, I knew Dad preferred me to the boys. There was something about the way he would ruffle my hair or swing me round. He never did that with them. He always seemed to relate better to girls than boys; that was just his nature.

When we were getting ready for school, having our breakfast, he would have a big gulp out of his mug of tea, a huge bite of toast (it seemed huge to me) and then rush off to work, giving me a kiss as he flew out. Only me. Not Mum. Not my brothers.

Dad – Francis, or Frank as everyone called him – was a carpenter. A good one. He worked a lot for Wimpey, making new homes. He was a tall, handsome, funny Irishman. Back then, he was always cheerful, but it wasn't long before he began to change. He was one of thirteen children, one of the older ones. There were five boys and the rest were sisters. I don't see much of that side of my family any more, only really Pat, my dad's sister, my godmother. The rest of them, they took Dad's side when our family fell apart.

Dad's parents had brought their family over from Ireland, but his dad didn't like it in Bristol and went back home after a while. My grandparents got divorced, which was a big thing, as they were very strong Catholics. So you would have thought that Dad's family might have been more supportive and understanding of Mum when everything went so wrong with her and Dad.

My mum, Maureen, didn't work. How could she? She had four kids to bring up, and a lot more to put up with. She was a great seamstress, though, and used to make curtains before she met Dad. She made clothes for us sometimes. I never liked them. It wasn't that they weren't pretty, but they were home-made and I felt everyone knew that. They were our 'best', for Sunday school and parties, but they didn't make me feel special. And I liked to feel special. When she produced identical outfits for Dawn and me to wear, I hated that.

But not as much as I hated it when Dawn got something new and I didn't. Her bright-red suit with the shiny buttons and matching hat I remember to this day. Normally we were dressed the same, but Mum decided to give Dawn a treat on the day of my First Communion. I was dressed traditionally in white; she was a picture. They all said so. As we were preparing to leave home, she twirled and giggled and laughed around the front room, thrilled with her new outfit. Everyone agreed she looked adorable, except me. I felt nothing but jealousy and bitterness.

After Dawn was born, I stopped being the little princess. I blamed her. It wasn't Dawn's fault, of course, but that didn't matter to me. We became close friends eventually, but it took a long time.

Not only did I like to feel special, I also liked to get my own way. I was a very determined little girl and that stubborn streak has never left me. When I set my heart on something, I will go to any lengths to make it happen. It is almost an illness. My body shuts down, reason takes flight and I am overcome with the need to get what I want. My brain doesn't function properly until I do. It hasn't always stood me in very good stead. In fact, it's led me to do things that were wrong, things I'm ashamed of. A lot of them.

All that is a long way off from the six-year-old girl who went shopping with her mother and siblings and saw a beautiful blue-and-white teddy bear sitting on a shelf. I had never seen anything like it in my life. I had to have it. When Mum, not surprisingly, said no, that was it. I screamed, I shouted, I tore at my clothes, I wailed, I fell to the ground, slapping my hands on the floor, writhing as though the Devil had possessed me.

At first, Mum tried to ignore my tantrum. Then she shouted at me and eventually she tried to reason with me. Shaun, Kevin and Dawn had seen it all before and wandered off to look at other toys. They couldn't care less if I was making a scene in public. Mum could, and eventually, with the shopkeeper becoming increasingly agitated because other customers were heading for the door, she gave in. I still have that teddy. He has seen a thing or two since then. Perhaps that little girl isn't so far in the past after all.

Until I was about seven, we were happy at home. We used to go on holiday to North Wales, around Llandudno, where Mum's family came from. She had two brothers and a sister. We would go over on the ferry from Bristol, the whole family, sometimes with my cousin Tina, who was Mum's sister Sonia's girl, and we would all play outside, run around, eat ice cream – normal stuff. Dad would act daft and make me laugh and laugh.

We lived in a house in Yate, on the outskirts of Bristol. That wasn't where I was born, but it's the first house I remember. It was a semi, with a small garden you entered through a gate. A path led up to the front door and into the hallway. There were three bedrooms. Dawn and I slept in one, my brothers in another and Mum and Dad in the big one. Out back, the garden was quite large and in summer we played there. Mum would watch us from the kitchen window.

The outside was painted white. Inside, there were carpets in every room. Net curtains hung from the windows and I remember the sills were painted peach. I used to pretend that if I licked them they tasted of the fruit. Dad would laugh at things like that.

He made me a doll's house for Christmas. It was my pride and joy. Everything was handmade. Mum did the curtains and the blankets for the beds and Dad carved everything else. It had two storeys, with an open front and a red-tiled covering on the roof. There were beds, chairs, minute kitchen implements, a television and wooden people, whom I adored. I would have loved the house anyway – it was beautiful – but Dad taking the time to build it for me, that made it extra special. I kept it safely in our bedroom. We were a happy family then, living in a happy home.

Some time in the early '70s, something changed. Dad always liked to go out to the pub – he enjoyed socialising – but it was becoming more and more regular, and he was beginning to drink heavily. He used to smell funny: alcohol. I didn't like it at first, but soon it became 'Dad's smell'. I got used to it and even grew to like it.

On a Saturday, he would go to the local at lunchtime and come back late in the afternoon for his tea. They must have had a lock-in, because the pubs shut at 2.30 p.m. back then. There was a crowd of regulars he met up with, so I guess the landlord kept the drinks flowing for them.

Sometimes he would arrive home in a good mood. He would bring us packets of crisps and bottles of Coke with straws. That would be our Saturday night treat, watching *Candid Camera* on the telly. Other times, though, it was different. He would appear in a black temper. No treats, just silent and moody, cursing at the television as he watched the football results come in, his pools coupon grasped firmly in his hand. He wasn't a big gambler, not as far as I know, but he sometimes needed extra money and that was his way of trying to get it fast. He had other expenses we didn't know anything about then. When he was like that, we all hid. There was no laughing. No *Candid Camera*. Even Mum kept out of his way.

Some Saturdays, and Fridays too, he didn't come home at all. He'd be gone all weekend. He never said where he'd been. He used to tell Mum that he was going out drinking and would be back when he was back. I missed him when that happened, but we could at least laugh in the house. And Mum seemed more relaxed, happier, when he wasn't around. I could always tell because she would take time to sit down, rest her feet on a footstool and read her book.

This went on for about a year: the mood swings, the tempers, the disappearing and occasionally the treats from the pub. He was never consistent, apart from in one aspect: he clearly loved Dawn and me very much. We were his little girls, and even though he would shout at us when we did something naughty or made noise or disturbed him when he was watching the football results, you could tell he never really meant it. There would always be a cuddle or a smile soon after, as if to say sorry.

For the boys, it was very different.

It was a Saturday morning. Dad hadn't come home the previous evening and when he did eventually walk through the door, he and Mum had a terrible row.

'You can't keep doing this, Frank. You can't. It's not fair on me. It's not fair on the children.'

We could all hear it but stayed out of the way. We had listened to this type of argument a lot recently and it was better if we disappeared upstairs, out of sight.

The next thing we knew, the four of us were being bundled into the car. Dad was taking Mum to visit a friend and we were too young to be left in the house on our own. We dropped Mum off and were heading home along the motorway, with us kids mucking around in the back seat, seeing who could be first to spot the next red car, that sort of thing, when suddenly Dad pulled over onto the hard shoulder. 'Right, you lot. I've got to go somewhere for a bit. But I'll be able to see the car the whole time. No one sets foot outside, you understand? Don't even open a door. I'll know if you do. And I won't be happy.' With that, he was off, leaving us sitting scared stiff as lorries whizzed by, shaking the car.

I don't know where he went that day. There were houses nearby, an estate, and I think he must have known there was a pub there. He came back about an hour later and he had that funny smell on him again. And he was angry. Ever so angry.

'Which one of you was it?' he bawled in our faces as he threw open the back door. 'I saw one of you get out when I told you not to move. Who was it? Who was it? Tell me now or you're all in for it!'

I started to cry. 'Daddy, it was Kevin.' It wasn't true; no one had got out. But I wanted him to stop shouting. I was frightened. I knew instantly it was a horrid, mean thing to do, but it was too late.

'You little bastard!' he screamed at Kevin. 'When you get home, you are going straight to your room. I'll deal with you there.' We all burst into tears. Kevin tried to defend himself, but Dad told him to shut up. No one said another word.

When we got home, Kevin was marched up to his room. Dad slammed the door behind them both. I can remember Kevin screaming that he had done as he was told, stayed in the car. Then I heard a slap, and then another.

'Daddy! Daddy!' I shouted from the bottom of the stairs. 'He didn't do it. He didn't. I'm sorry. He didn't do anything.'

Kevin's screaming stopped. All I could hear then was crying and more slaps.

When Dad came out, his face was red and he was breathing heavily. 'He's not leaving that room until he says sorry.' Kevin was a tough little boy and I knew he wouldn't apologise for something he hadn't done, so I crept up to his room while Dad was fixing some lunch.

'Kevin, I didn't mean it. It just came out. I'm sorry, I'm sorry, I'm sorry.'

'That's OK, Laura. I know. It's not your fault.'

'Please say you're sorry to Dad. Please. He's still so angry. He'll lock you in here all day. If you say you're sorry, Daddy will be happy again. It'll be best.'

Later, when Dad went up to see him, Kevin must have apologised, because he was allowed out. He must have hated saying sorry. He always understood the difference between right and wrong, and I was proud of him for being so brave.

The violence began to get worse.

A Saturday night. Dad had been in the pub all afternoon and when he eventually staggered home Mum said she was going to her sister Sonia's for the evening. I think she had become frightened of his temper and thought it was better to stay out of the way when he was like that. Off she went on the bus and we were sent to bed early. Later that night, about 11 p.m., I guess, Dad's shouting woke me.

He had bolted the front door so Mum couldn't get in. He'd been sitting downstairs drinking all evening and had fallen asleep in his chair. When Mum found she was unable to open the door, she knocked loudly. He was using horrible, nasty words.

'You fucking bitch, waking me up! You worthless tramp!'

'Calm down, Frank,' I could hear Mum pleading through the letter box. 'You'll wake the children. Please let me in and we can talk.'

The bolts were pulled back and the door opened.

'Where the hell have you been? You selfish bitch, leaving me to look after your kids because you don't care.' Then there was a heavy thump.

'Stop, Frank, please! Not again. Please.'

A thud.

'Pleeease, Frank.'

I knew he was hitting her. I curled into a ball under my blanket, wishing with all my little heart that the noise would stop. I don't know if Dawn or the boys were awake. We never talked about it, but they must have been. No one could sleep through that.

I drifted off again. By then, I had grown too big for my little bunk, so Dawn and I had graduated to single beds alongside each other. The crack of light coming through the bedroom door as it was gently opened made me sit up, confused and sleepy. It was Mum, still wearing her clothes.

'Shh, love,' she murmured. 'There's nothing to worry about. It's just me. Back to sleep, now. I'm going to cuddle up next to you tonight.' She quietly slipped into the bed, put her arms around me and as I snuggled in I could smell the familiar smoke on her hair and feel the wetness of tears on her cheeks.

I wasn't there when Mum first became suspicious that my father was having an affair, but she told me about it later. In between the drunken rages, the violence and the disappearing acts, she and Dad did have some good times. When he wanted, he could be charming, good company and very popular. On those occasions, Mum was proud to have him on her arm. But those times became less and less frequent and eventually non-existent.

During one of the good spells, Dad took Mum to a social event at a caravan park not far from where we lived. It was one of those parks where a lot of the sites are permanent, with families living there. The residents used to throw parties in the amenity centre and these were open to guests from outside. This one was a big do. We had a babysitter and Mum and Dad had dressed up to the nines. Dawn and I were allowed to stay up so we could see them before they left. Mum looked beautiful. Dad looked happy, smiling and joking. If only life could always have been like this.

At the party, they were sitting with a group at a table, the couple they had gone with plus other friends of my father's, people he seemed to know well, from the pub, Mum assumed. She was introduced to a woman at the party. Her name was Jose. This woman was laughing, drinking and seemed at ease with the crowd. In particular, she was paying Dad a lot of attention. While Mum was chatting away, she noticed the husband of the couple they were with lean across and tap Dad on the shoulder. It was one of those moments when the conversation in a crowd dips for no reason and you can hear what otherwise would have been drowned out. 'You're in there, Frank,' the man slurred, drunkenly nudging Dad in the ribs.

'Shut up,' was Dad's reply. It was enough for Mum to begin to worry, but not enough for her actually to confront Dad. I don't think it would have made any difference if she had. By then, things were too far gone.

By the spring bank holiday weekend, at the end of May 1973, many months after the caravan park party, life at home had become unbearable for Mum. Not that I realised it at the time. I knew there had been a lot of rows and shouting recently, and sometimes I would hear Mum creep down the stairs to sleep on the sofa, but what I hadn't understood was that the situation had escalated to the point where my life was about to change for ever. The tension only arose when Dad was home, and a lot of the time he wasn't. Like on this Saturday morning.

Something was clearly wrong. Mum was agitated and she hadn't allowed any of us to go out and play, even though the sun was shining. 'Stay in,' she told us. 'Do as I say.'

A car pulled up outside the house. It was Patrick, Mum's brother. He didn't come round very often. Mum called us all together. 'Everybody listen. We're leaving, right now. We're going to stay with Sonia. I don't want any complaints.'

A black cloud of worry enveloped us kids. We were confused and, in my panic, I didn't think Mum was including me. 'Mummy, Mummy, can I come too? Don't leave me, please.'

'Of course I'm not leaving you, darling. But we've all got to go now. Come on.'

'Can I bring my –'

'There's no time to bring anything. We can pick up your toys another day. Come on.'

Everyone was rushing around and I couldn't find my shoes. My wellies were in the kitchen, so I put them on, helped Dawn with hers and we were off. When the door closed behind us, that was it. We never lived there again as a family.

Within a year, blood was spilt in that house – and I was a witness.

Chapter Two
Daddy, I Want to Go Home

'Oh God, the car isn't there. Where are they? Patrick, where are they?'

Even as a six year old, I could recognise the panic in Mum's voice. We had escaped, we had come to live at Mum's sister Sonia and her husband Andy's flat and they weren't home.

'Don't worry, Maureen,' Patrick said, trying to reassure her, 'they'll just be out at the shops or something. I'll go and double check. You stay here with the kids.' He was back in no time. 'No answer. But I'm sure they won't be long. Let's wait a bit.'

'But what if they're away for the weekend, Patrick? I can't go back. I can't. I don't know what he'll do.'

Sitting in the back of the car, I knew that the 'he' was Dad. Mum was scared and that made me scared. Beside me, Dawn, Shaun and Kevin sat rigid, saying nothing, staring straight ahead. We were all frightened. What minutes ago had seemed like an adventure wasn't fun any more.

It was warm, so we got out of the car and stood watching Sonia's front door, wishing with everything we had that she would appear from around the corner. We must have looked a sight: four kids, two in wellington boots on a hot summer's day, standing by the side of the road, holding hands, pale and shivering because we all knew something bad was happening, with Mum chain-smoking and Patrick pacing up and down, peeking through Sonia's window as if that would make her miraculously reappear. We had no toys to play with, so we milled around aimlessly. Mum was too agitated to speak. Dawn began to cry. So did I. The boys remained brave, trying to be men. I loved them for that.

'We can't stay here, Patrick. He'll be home by now. He'll come looking for us. He might drive past. He'll see us. We have to go.'

'Come on, then. Back to mine. We'll check again in an hour or so.'

Patrick's house wasn't far and when we got there his wife, Audrey, made Mum tea and gave us kids some juice and a sandwich. Even though we were scared, we were always hungry. Patrick and Audrey had two children of their own, who were lovely, but, sitting there, in their living room, no one spoke very much. All I can remember hearing over and over again was, 'It'll be all right, Maureen. It'll be all right. He won't come here.'

'But he'll kill me if I have to go back.'

After what seemed for ever but was probably no more than an hour, less even, Patrick said, 'Come on, Shaun, come with me. We'll walk over and see if anyone's home.' Off they went, with Mum calling after them, 'For God's sake, don't get seen. Please be careful.'

We sat there, with the air filling with smoke even though the windows were wide open, all eyes on the door. Within minutes, we heard the 'slap, slap, slap' of a boy's trainers on the path outside. Shaun burst into the hallway and breathlessly announced, 'They're back.'

Mum rang Sonia's doorbell. We were crowded behind her. The door opened. 'Sonia, we need somewhere to sleep.'

I know we were family, but, even still, Sonia and Andy were amazing. They obviously knew that Mum had been unhappy, perhaps they knew even more, but Mum hadn't told them she was leaving Dad. We were a complete surprise arriving on the doorstep as we did, but Sonia beckoned us in with a broad smile.

'Come into the kitchen, Maureen,' she said. 'Tell me what's

going on.' The door was shut, so I couldn't hear what was being said. We crowded into the tiny hallway, not wanting to intrude until everything was settled. When Mum reappeared, the relief was clear on her face. Holding tightly to her sister's hand, she simply said, 'We're staying.'

Later that evening, just before bed, something exciting and bewildering happened. Sonia asked us all, 'Now, what would you lot like for some supper?' I had no idea what she was talking about. What was 'supper'? I had never heard of it before. Sonia's kids all yelled out 'Chipsticks!', so I said the same: 'Em, Chipsticks, please.' This was living – being allowed a snack before bed. It's the best day ever, I thought. A child's view of the world can change very rapidly.

Our house in Yate had hardly been spacious, but in comparison we had been rattling around in there. Sonia and Andy lived in a small two-bedroom ground-floor flat and they had three kids, two boys and a girl. There was no way it could accommodate us all and it was agreed that Shaun and Kevin would stay with Patrick and Audrey for a while. Even with them gone, there was still a lot of sorting to do if everyone was to be fitted in. Dawn, Mum and I shared a room, Mum in one single bed and the two of us top to tail in the other – for the first night. I didn't like sharing with Dawn, so after that I made her sleep with Mum, who was too worn out to fight my selfishness. Sonia's oldest, Tina, slept on the sofa in the lounge and the two boys with their parents.

Despite the cramped conditions, it was a generally happy household. Shaun and Kevin would come round often to visit and the fact that Mum was less tense made all the difference. She smiled more and we felt safe. It was our sanctuary from the drunken unpredictability, bouts of violence, sullen moods and angry arguments that home life had been for too long. Dad was never mentioned.

In the evenings, our bedroom became the 'kids' den'. While Mum, Sonia and Andy were watching television, we would congregate there playing games or listening to pop songs that

Tina had taped off the radio on her portable cassette recorder. The quality was terrible, but that didn't matter. We would have a whole C90 of songs from the charts, and we would dance around and sing. My favourite was 'Tie a Yellow Ribbon Round the Ole Oak Tree'. I loved that song and asked for it to be repeated again and again. On Thursdays, *Top of the Pops* was the big treat and at the weekends we would be allowed to watch television with the adults. Being able to sit happily watching *Dad's Army* while Sonia brushed my hair, and not being afraid to talk or make a noise, was so different. It seemed like a new world to us, although I didn't realise at the time that alcohol continued to be a presence in my life. By then, Sonia was drinking heavily in the evenings, cider mainly. From my child's point of view, it was nothing more than a drink that made her happy, but it proved to be a constant burden she carried with her as the years passed.

One Saturday morning, I was sitting alone on the front doorstep. The other kids were off playing in the sunshine, but I hadn't wanted to go. I was in a sulk. Dawn had said something funny at breakfast and everyone had laughed. She was only four, but the attention she'd received had annoyed me, made me jealous. So I decided I had better be in a huff. No one really noticed, which made it all the worse. Sonia and Mum were in the kitchen. I could hear them talking.

'I've had a letter,' Mum was saying. 'It's from Frank. He says, "Please come home. I miss my girls. I want to see them." Bloody typical. He doesn't mention Shaun or Kevin. Or me.'

'You'll have to reply. You know that, don't you? You can't hide from him for ever. Will you go back?'

'Never, Sonia. Never, ever. I can't. I won't.'

'What about the girls? He is their dad.'

'I know. If he wants to see Laura and Dawn, I'm not sure I can stop that. And if I tried, he could get nasty. You know him. I'll write.'

I was awake very early the next day, Sunday, thinking about what Mum had said. Daddy wanted to see me. I didn't know how I felt. Excited, frightened, confused. All those things. I got up. Everyone was still asleep. I picked up my clothes from the little chair where I'd thrown them the night before and crept out of the room and out of the flat. I ran across the road and into the local church. No one was around, but the door was open. I stopped in front of it, wary. But then I thought of Dad, gritted my teeth and went in.

I didn't usually get up early. Ever since we'd arrived at Sonia's, I had taken to lying in bed on a Sunday morning, listening to the bells ringing in this church. They made me sad. When we were with Dad in Yate, we used to go to Sunday school. I liked it. It was fun and going into the church was comforting somehow. But as the arguments raged in our house and things became horrid, we stopped going. The bells made me think of that and I hated them. Sunday school had been when we were a family; not going was when everything began to go wrong.

The bells conjured images of Dad. What was he doing? Was he going to church again now that we weren't there to bother him? I missed him. I couldn't help it. When he'd had his happy face on, he'd been so loving to me. He made me feel special, even though Dawn had taken the shine off that to some extent. Living as we were, there was no room for anyone to be singled out. I understood that, but it didn't mean that in my quiet moments I didn't long to be made to feel different. Only Dad could do that.

It was cold in the church, even though it was summertime. I stood looking at the altar for a moment and then padded quietly to the tower. I gently tugged on a bell rope. It hardly moved. I tried harder and harder and harder, pulling on that rope with what little strength I had. It hurt my hands, but I kept going and slowly it moved and then I heard it. The bell began to ring. With the momentum of the bell swinging far above me, it became easier and soon the rings were loud. Could Daddy hear me? Daft, really, as Yate was miles away, but I hoped he could.

After perhaps a minute, I let go. I was tired and worried I would be punished if anyone came to investigate. I darted out and back across the road. I hadn't been missed, although the ringing had clearly woken someone up, as I could hear noises in the bathroom. I slipped my shoes off and pretended to be reading my book when Andy came into the kitchen. I didn't tell anyone I had been out.

Ringing the bells became a regular thing for me over that summer. Eventually, the church warden caught me. She lay in wait one Sunday to see who was doing it. I was in a bit of trouble, but mainly Mum thought it was just a little girl's silly prank. It had become much more than that for me, though. I had been reaching out for my father. And it seemed he heard, because not long after I was caught Dad came to pick Dawn and me up.

The summer was coming to an end. Mum had arranged for us to attend the local school in Patchway. Dawn was to go to infants, Kevin and I to the junior school and Shaun to the senior school. In registering us at the new school, Mum had been required to explain why we were transferring from Yate and that had prompted a visit to social services.

I was sitting in a room in a big building. Mum was with me. There wasn't much on the walls, just posters with children looking sad and something about hair lice. Yeuch, was all I could think as the nice lady spoke to me.

'Now, Laura, you are not in any trouble. You have done nothing wrong. Please don't be frightened.' I was immediately frightened and thought I had done something wrong. 'I know your mummy and daddy don't live in the same house any more. How does that make you feel?'

'I like it at Sonia's.'

'Good. Lovely. Now, your daddy misses you. Do you miss him?'

I didn't know what to say. I looked at Mum. She smiled. 'It's OK, Laura.'

'I . . . I miss Daddy sometimes.' I started to cry.

'That's fine, Laura. You're doing so well. You're very brave. Only one more question. Do you want to go and live with your daddy?'

'No, no, I don't. I don't. He shouts sometimes. And we never have supper.'

A few days before the beginning of term, Mum explained that Sonia, Andy and the kids had found a new place to live. It was up the road, a three-bedroom house. They were moving and we were staying in the flat. Shaun and Kevin were coming home. The council had agreed for the tenancy to be passed to Mum, although that meant nothing to me at the time.

I was sorry when they moved out, even though we had been living on top of each other. It had felt safe living there, and mostly fun, although towards the end some of us kids had begun to squabble, so I suspect the adults were pleased with how things turned out. Once we'd settled into our new routine, I especially loved it when I was allowed to watch the television programmes I liked. Dawn was always happy to go along with me. *Sesame Street* and *The Clangers* used to make me laugh and laugh.

My new school looked perfectly nice, but I didn't want to go. On the first morning, I refused even to put on my uniform. On the second, I clung to Mum's leg so tightly she couldn't prise me off. This went on all the first week, because after that second day I heard Mum speaking to a friend, admitting, 'I can't get her out of the house.' That was all I needed to hear. It was the blue-and-white teddy situation all over again: I had won. But, of course, I hadn't really. Mum was too smart. She sat down with me at the kitchen table the following Monday morning. 'Laura, you have to go today or they'll take you away from me. For ever.' That did it.

Not long after I started going to the school, Mum came into our bedroom to explain something to Dawn and me. 'Your father wants to see you and I have been asked to let him. Does that upset or worry either of you?' We both shook our heads. 'Good girls. He's going to come tomorrow after school, in his car. He'll pick you up and take you back to where we used to live. You can have something to eat there and then he'll bring you home. Laura, bring your teddy, and, Dawn, you bring your dolly.'

When Dad's car pulled up outside the flat the following day, we were both still in our school uniforms. Mum had brushed our hair and made us wash our faces. There was no way we were going to show her up. Dad didn't come in. He waited outside. When Mum opened the door to take us out, I pulled back. Suddenly, I was frightened. I was excited as well, but what if this was like when we left Yate? Would we ever come back to Mummy? Tears followed, from both me and Dawn.

'Mummy, I don't want to never see you ever again. Mummy!'

She crouched down and held us both close. 'Don't worry, darlings. Mummy will be here when you come back. Your father will bring you home. I promise.'

And that was it. The next thing we knew, we were in the back of Dad's car and heading back to Yate. I think Dad must have been nervous about the visit, because he hardly spoke. He said how smart we looked and how much he had missed us, that was all. He never mentioned the boys. He didn't want to see them and they didn't want to see him.

When we arrived at our old house, it looked the same from the outside. Same front door, same net curtains in the windows. But it was different inside. There was a new family there.

'Laura, Dawn, this is Jose. She lives here.' I couldn't believe what I was seeing. Who was this? What was she doing here? Why had no one said anything? The woman standing in front of us had long blonde hair and wore glasses. She was nothing like Mum. And she was holding a baby of about 18 months. 'And this is Frankie,' said Dad. 'He lives here too.'

At that moment, two other young lads appeared, about three and four years old, crashing past us in the hallway, charging upstairs, shouting at each other and bursting through the door to what had been our room. I didn't like them from that moment, and I never grew to.

How could Daddy have a new family? Weren't we good enough? Was it my fault for saying I wanted to stay with Mum? I was so confused. I held on to Dawn's hand as Dad led us through to the kitchen, past the familiar pictures on the wall, past the television we used to watch, past the sofa and chairs we used to sit on – all the same but totally alien.

Jose left us with Dad for most of the visit and after an hour or so he said it was time to leave. He had asked about school and how Tina was, but never once did he mention Kevin, Shaun or Mum.

Mum was waiting by the front door when we got home. Before we had even got our coats off, she started: 'Well? What was it like? Has anything changed? What did your father ask? Who was there? Did he say anything about what he was doing?'

'Daddy has got some new children. He doesn't love us any more,' I said, and then I explained about Jose and the others.

'So they've moved in,' Mum sighed. 'Frankie is his son,' she told us.

Mum had already discovered the truth about Jose and Frankie. On the Tuesday after the bank holiday weekend during which we'd escaped, Mum had visited her local councillor. She needed to explain that she had split up from Dad and that she had four children and would need somewhere to live. Back then, going to your councillor was the quickest way to sort something like that out. She went on to say that Dad would be living in the house on his own.

The councillor was a friend of Dad's through the church. He was confused. 'Hold on a second. I don't understand. Frank doesn't live there. He lives at the caravan park.'

'What do you mean?'

'I really don't think I should say any more. This is a private domestic matter – none of my business.'

And that was it; he clammed up. But Mum was on the warpath. Off she went to the caravan park and spoke to the site manager. 'I believe Mr Walsh is here. I want to know where he is and who he's living with.'

More confusion. 'Who the hell are you?' the manager asked.

'Tell me who he's living with and then I'll tell you who I am.'

'Why is it any of your business?'

'Because I am Mrs Walsh. His wife.'

'You can't be. Mrs Walsh is here with Mr Walsh.'

'And what is "Mrs Walsh's" name?'

'Jose Walsh. She had a baby a year or so ago.'

Suddenly, it all fell into place. Mum felt like a fool, an idiot. The nights away, the embarrassed 'shut up' at the party. Her husband had been living a double life with a second family. She never forgave him.

The visits to Dad's continued throughout that autumn and into the winter. Sometimes, I didn't want to go back and would cling to Mum in the hallway when he arrived to pick us up. Mum would eventually persuade me that it was all OK, but Dad would know I hadn't wanted to see him. 'That's your mother, that mad woman, poisoning you against me,' he'd say. 'Don't listen to her. She just wants to hurt me.' I hated it when he talked about Mum like that.

The one huge bonus for me when we were at Dad's was Frankie. I loved him and would spend my whole time playing with him, picking him up, cuddling him and singing him songs. There was something wonderful, beautiful and innocent about him. Even then, I knew I wanted one of my own.

It was a lovely spring evening. Dad was driving us home. We were happy. Frankie had been wailing when we'd arrived, but I'd gone straight over and tickled his nose as he lay on the sofa. He'd stopped crying and begun laughing. I'd picked him up and he'd made a contented gurgle. 'She loves babies,' Dad had said to Jose. She smiled. Dawn and I had had fun playing with Frankie before he went to bed; we'd had tea; Jose had even asked us about school. I'd forgotten to mention I was going to be in an Easter play. We'd talked about painting hard-boiled eggs the following week. It had been one of the best ever visits.

On the way home, Dad told us stories about when he was growing up with all his brothers and sisters. Dawn and I giggled when he described the naughty things they'd got up to. Outside the flat, Mum was waiting for us as usual. Dad drove down the street and swung the car round, as he always did, so he could pull up on our side of the road. The passenger window was down because the weather had begun to improve.

Mum usually opened the door for us, but this time she leaned in the front window first. This was a surprise. They hardly ever spoke to each other. The engine was still running; Dad never wanted to linger.

'Frank, the girls can't come next week. Laura's in a show at school.'

Dad flipped. I had never seen anything like it. 'What the hell are you telling me now for? We have plans. You can't do this. You have no right! I'm not letting you.'

With that, he slammed his foot down on the accelerator and we were gone. I turned round to look out of the back window. Mum was chasing the car down the street. Through the open window, I could hear her screaming, 'Give me my girls back! Give them back!'

What was happening? 'Daddy, I want to go home. Daddy!'

He was quite calm. 'We are going home, Laura. You're staying with me now.'

Chapter Three
Tiny Tears Can Come Too

I stood staring at my beloved doll's house. It was ruined. Throughout our previous visits, I had been too intimidated by Jose's boys to ask to play with it. I knew it was still in their room. All I could think to do was ask God to look after my cherished wooden family. Standing there, it was clear He hadn't listened, and it was my fault. Why would God pay any attention to me now that I no longer attended Sunday school?

The chairs were smashed, the carpet ripped, the tiled covering peeling off the roof and the people broken in two. The loss I felt was unbearable and I wept for hours, in an unfamiliar room that had once been pretty; the ripped wallpaper and crayon scribbles now offered no comfort. When we'd arrived back from Mum's, Jose's boys had moved out of our room and had given it back to us, but it was no longer home.

The next morning, I listened to Dad on the telephone. 'I've already explained to someone in your department. The girls told me last night that they didn't want to stay at their mother's any more. They're unhappy there and at their school. They want to stay with me . . . Yes, I understand. Of course you have to send someone round to make sure everything's OK.'

To this day, I don't understand how a simple phone call to social services was sufficient for us to be taken away from Mum to live with Dad. But that is what happened. A social worker did eventually come round to check up, but it was weeks later, even though Mum had been onto them that same morning trying to get us back. By the time we were seen by the authorities, Dad had us in a local Yate school and to a large extent we were settled. Kids learn to survive no matter what. We both missed Mum and Shaun and Kevin, but now we were with Dad and he loved us. That felt good, particularly for me.

Dad was treating me as his special one again. I had to go to bed at the same time as Dawn and Jose's two older boys, but once Dawn was asleep I was allowed to come back downstairs and sit on Dad's lap while he watched television. I loved doing that. It was a secret and that made it all the better.

Over the previous months, I had noticed Jose getting fatter but had paid it little attention. On our visits, we had rarely spoken to her, which had suited both Dawn and me fine. Now that we were living in the same house, everything was different, but I still didn't mention her weight.

We came home from school one day and Dad was waiting. Normally, Jose was there at that time. 'She's in hospital,' Dad explained. 'She's had a baby. You'll see him in a day or so.' I didn't understand how it had happened, but I was excited. A new baby! I couldn't wait and when I first saw the little bundle I was besotted. Joseph was his name and he had the most beautiful, tiny wrinkly hands, a snub nose, loads of hair and a smile that went right through me. He was the most incredible thing I had ever seen and when I picked him up and smelled his skin it was heaven. I adored looking after Frankie and Joseph.

Dawn and I both missed Mum, and I know she did everything she could to get us back. She went to the council, wrote letters, made phone calls. She even went to the police, but they just viewed the fact that Dad had in effect kidnapped us as a domestic issue, nothing to do with them. I don't think she bothered going to the local councillor. She probably thought that would have been a waste of time.

The problem for Mum was that when social services did

eventually come round, they gave a glowing report of our new set-up. Every subsequent report was the same. The fresh smell of polish, disinfectant and soap was apparently no indication that Dad somehow knew of their imminent arrival in advance. On each occasion they were due, you could feel the tension in the house rising and a major spring-cleaning operation was undertaken, with Dad instructing us all to wash everything twice, including ourselves.

Why didn't we say anything? I think Dawn and I were both too afraid of the repercussions. With all the upheaval we had endured, I know I felt incredibly insecure, and I didn't want to make the situation any worse. If I said I wanted to be back with Mum, what would Dad think? How would he react? Would we be thrown out immediately? He would be upset and I didn't want to be responsible for making him sad. It is very hard to speak up when you know your father loves you and you love him, even if deep down you also know you shouldn't be with him.

Dad was still drinking heavily. At the weekends, he was still spending most lunchtimes in the pub, and he'd go again at night. During the week, if I was downstairs with him, he would always have a drink on the go. Sometimes when Dad had been in the pub at lunchtime, he would come back in a foul mood. Dawn and I would recognise it the moment he walked in and quickly escape to our room to play. Even though he never raised a hand to either of us, we didn't want to be shouted at or told to sit still and do nothing.

Neither Dawn nor I had seen or spoken to Mum since the day Dad had driven off with us. Actually, that is not entirely true. We did see her about a week after we arrived in Yate. During that initial period, when she was pursuing with the authorities every possibility to have us returned, with no success, she decided to take matters into her own hands. She tried to snatch us back. Given what Dad might have done if he had caught her, it was an incredibly brave thing to do.

Dad must have suspected she would try something, because

from day one he had told me that I was not to speak to Mum, that the police would arrest me if I did, because it was now his job to look after me. He was so serious that I nodded, wide-eyed and believing.

It was the Easter holidays. Dad was at work and I was out the front playing. Everyone else was inside. I heard a shout and when I looked up I saw Mum getting out of a car and running towards me.

'Laura! Laura, it's me, Mummy. Come here, love.'

I jumped up, took the first step to rush into her arms, then remembered the police. I had to do what Daddy had told me or there would be terrible trouble. I turned round and darted back through the front door.

'Jose, Mummy's outside!' I shouted.

'Shit! Frank will go mental. Quick, Laura, lock the door.'

I did as I was told, then jumped onto the sofa, where Jose was sitting with Dawn. I could hear Mum banging on the front door.

'Open this door! Open this door! I want my daughters back. Give me my girls. I know you're in there. Give them back!'

She stopped, and I could hear her footsteps moving away. Jose lit a cigarette. Mum's face appeared at the front window. She was stooping down, peering through the gap in the net curtains. She had been crying. Jose put her arms round us both and continued to smoke.

'Laura, please open the door,' Mum called. 'It's time to come home.'

I wanted to go to her, but I couldn't move. Dad would be upset with me if I opened the door, but at the same time I wanted a cuddle from Mummy. I didn't know what to do for the best, so I did nothing. I think Dawn was in shock. She didn't say a word, didn't cry; she just sat staring at Mum and sucking her thumb.

It felt as though Mum was at the window for hours, but she can't have been. Minutes, I suppose. The last thing she said was, 'I'll come back for you, girls. I'll never leave you. I promise. I'll never stop trying to get you back.' Her heart must have been breaking.

We heard a door slam and a car drive off. Jose went to the window, checked outside and then produced a clothes catalogue for me to look through, so I could pick an outfit for Joseph's christening. I think she was attempting to divert my attention, but it didn't work. Normally, I would have loved the opportunity to choose whatever I wanted, but as Jose flicked through the pages with me, all I could see was Mum's face at the window. I pointed out a smart grey and pink suit that I liked, but it gave me no pleasure. When Dad returned home and Jose told him what had happened, he said only one thing: 'That bitch.'

Mum obviously did keep trying, because it wasn't too long before Dad told us he was taking us to see her. He'd received a legal letter insisting that Mum had visiting rights. He wasn't happy about having to take us, but he must have known that if he didn't he would lose us entirely.

'I'm taking you to see your slag of a mother. She's forced the police into making me do it. I want you to tell your mother how much you like living here, how much you like school. It's important. Your mother will say lots of nasty things about me, but they won't be true. She's changed. She isn't like she used to be. That's why I took you away, so you could be safe here. Don't listen to the bitch. I know you don't want to go, but you have to. I am sorry, honeys. I'll come and pick you up again as soon as I can.'

After he told us that, we didn't know what to think. Before, everything at Mum's had been safe and calm. Was it all different now? I knew things weren't right here, at Dad's, but would they be worse at Mum's? Had she changed? I wanted to see her, but I was scared. Most of the time, I wished we were living with Mum. But now? Maybe it was better here. I just didn't know. But if Daddy was going to protect me, then everything would be OK.

All the way in the car the next day I kept saying, 'I am not going. I am not going,' over and over again. Dad eventually became exasperated. 'For God's sake, Laura, stop it. You are going and that's that. Remember what I told you. Now be a good girl for your daddy and keep quiet.'

When we pulled up outside Mum's flat, Dawn was out in a flash. Mum was standing by the front door and Dawn ran to her. The moment she had seen Mum, everything Dad had said was instantly forgotten. But not by me. I wouldn't move. After a few moments, Dad got out and walked round to the back door. He was going to make me get out. Then he was going to drive away, leaving me. I was convinced. I didn't want that. I was safe with him. And there was Joseph to look after. I couldn't leave Joseph. When he slammed the driver's door shut, his car keys made a jangling sound. Suddenly, I had a plan. I leaned forward between the two front seats, pulled the keys out of the ignition, and as Dad opened one door I shot out the other.

'You're not leaving me here. You're not. I won't let you!' I shouted as I ran into the house. I knew I had to see Mum – part of me wanted to, despite the worries Dad had fed me with – but I was going to make damn sure he would be there to take me back again. There was no way he was going to cross the threshold to retrieve his keys. For two hours, he sat outside in his car, waiting.

It must have torn Mum apart to have him out there, and to know that I hadn't wanted to come inside. Dawn had told her what I had been chanting in the car, but Mum didn't say anything. I think she wanted the visit to be as perfect as possible. It was incredible how strong she was.

We settled into an uneasy routine. During our visits to Mum, she would gently try to find out what was happening at Dad's, never trying to force the issue but always pushing for stories. Sometimes I would see tears in her eyes when she thought I wasn't looking. I found the trips unsettling, but whenever Mum gave me a hug, with the comforting smell of cigarettes on her breath, Mum's smell, I always felt better. There is nothing in the world like the hug of a mother, but it made me feel even more confused, because at Dad's there was almost no reassurance to be had.

His drinking was getting out of control – every night now. Rows and rages happened almost daily. There was one of those big, heavy pressure cookers in the kitchen that used to make a whistling noise out of the valve on the top. Life at Dad's had reached that high-pitched screeching point. Something had to give. We all knew it, I think.

'Dawn, Dawn, wake up,' I whispered, gently shaking my sister. I don't know what time it was, but it was still dark outside and the house was quiet. I had a little torch shaped like one of the characters from *Sesame Street*, and I shone it on Dawn as she sat up blinking and confused.

'I'm going to escape and you're coming with me. We're going to Mummy's.' I saw her startled eyes dart to her beloved doll lying next to her in bed. 'Tiny Tears can come too,' I reassured her.

'How are we . . .?'

'I've made a map. Look.' I handed it across to her. I'd been thinking about this for a while now, paying careful attention to the route to Mum's flat when I sat in the front of Dad's car as he drove us there. I knew you needed a map if you were going to escape. Of course you did. That was essential.

Dawn was impressed. 'When?'

'Ssh. Not so loud. We'll go tonight. Mummy will have clothes for us.'

According to my plan, we would walk all the way there in our nightdresses and arrive at Mum's in under an hour. Mum would be so pleased to see us we wouldn't be in trouble for being out past bedtime. Dawn, me and her dolly would be free from all the shouting. Everything was going to be all right again.

Only we didn't leave that night. Our whispers must have woken Dad, or perhaps he got up to go to the toilet, I don't know, but we heard him moving around and quickly climbed back into bed, torch off. The plan would have to wait another night or two. How I wish with all my heart that we had gone then.

Chapter Four

My Dad Is Dead

By this stage, Dad had taken to being in the pub most of the evening and my secret times with him had all but ended. I still hoped he might call me down and I tried to stay awake for as long as I could just in case. But in my heart I realised that drink had taken control of his life. He wasn't the same. He frequently flew into a rage. Out of respect for the privacy of Jose and her children, I have deliberately avoided giving much detail about this period, but suffice it to say that it was a frightening time for me and Dawn.

I am not sure if it was the night after I had planned our escape or the following one. In any case, Dawn and I were in bed. Dawn was asleep, but I was still awake, lying in misery in the darkness, mechanically pulling strands of my hair out, a habit that has been with me ever since in times of stress.

I heard him trying to get his key in the lock. I could hear the scraping of metal against metal as he kept failing to find the keyhole. Eventually, he stumbled through the door. He was angry and very drunk. I kept murmuring to myself, 'Please go to bed, Daddy. Please be good.' Sometimes I would tell myself that if I said these words to him it would all stop. Daddy would listen because he loved me. But I was too scared to do so. I believe now that he wouldn't have listened anyway; he was too far gone by that stage.

That night, the situation escalated. He attacked Jose, the police were called and she moved out. She left that night, taking her two boys and Joseph but not Frankie. Dad wouldn't let her take him.

Dawn and I were not allowed to stay, even though we wanted to. There was a nice policewoman who explained to us that until everything was sorted out we had to sleep somewhere else. Dad gave them the addresses of two of his sisters, Pat, my godmother, and Margaret. Dad called them and asked if they would look after us for a while. I went to Pat's and Dawn went with Margaret and her husband, Dave. Dad never mentioned Mum and we did what we were told.

My third bed in a matter of months. I felt lonely. I missed my sister. I missed my mum. I didn't even visit Mum while I was at Pat's. I think she was told that Dawn and I were off visiting relatives.

Pat was married to Ray. They were lovely and did everything they could to welcome me into their family, but it wasn't home. And it was hard on their kids. Suddenly, here was a cousin from out of the blue, taking all the attention. 'Poor little Laura.' 'What would Laura like?' 'How are you feeling today, Laura?' They didn't want me there and I didn't want to be there. I felt like an outsider, abandoned even, and my hair-pulling became even more intense. During one particularly violent evening thunderstorm, I became so disturbed and upset that I pulled out clumps and rolled them into a ball along with wool strands I had nervously plucked from the blanket on my bed. Pat was very concerned when she discovered this and started taking me to her work (she was a sewing machinist) to cheer me up. I was happier there, sitting amongst the rows of ladies as they laughed and joked, making a fuss of me.

After everything that had happened, I still wanted my daddy. A fortnight passed before my wish was granted and Dawn and I were allowed to go back to live with him.

So it was back to normal. Only it wasn't, because, with Jose gone, I had to look after my sister and my half-brother when Dad was out working. I was ten. School was out of the question, for both Dawn and me. If I couldn't go, neither could she. Dad must have said we had moved back to Patchway to be with Mum, because no one came to find out why we had suddenly stopped attending.

Dad was under a lot of pressure. Cash was becoming an issue. He had several children to support and finances were certainly preying on his mind, not that it stopped him drinking. He would leave early in the morning to go off to a job and it could be eight or nine at night before he reappeared in a haze of alcohol fumes. I had no problem looking after Frankie, and Dawn helped with the cooking, but I had no idea how to keep a house properly clean and tidy. I would use the little brush from the fire set to sweep the lounge and kitchen. Dad took all the dirty clothes to the launderette on Saturday mornings. He would wait there until they were washed and dried, bring them home, then it was off to the pub. I wouldn't say we were happy, but we got on with it. And we never said a word to Mum. Dad made sure of that.

'You know that programme you watch?' Dad said before he took us to see Mum for the first time since Jose had left. '*Magpie*, I think it's called.' We nodded. It was similar to *Blue Peter* and I liked them both. 'You know the song they sing?' he continued. 'One for sorrow, two for joy, three for a girl, four for a boy. Well, when you get to seven magpies, it means a secret never to be told, and that's like us. We've got a secret never to be told about Jose and school. You can never speak to your mother about any of that. OK? Promise? Good girls. Because if you do, seven magpies will die.' Dad was very clever sometimes. Like all little girls, we loved animals, and the thought of being responsible for killing any was too horrible to imagine.

Life couldn't go on like this, not indefinitely. Dad was becoming too unstable, increasingly desperate and paranoid. He became convinced that there would be a knock at the door at any moment and his girls and little boy would be taken away for ever. He knew there were too many loose strands to hold together. One of them was bound to slip free, and that would be the one that hanged him. Mum finding out that Jose had gone, the school making enquiries, social services undertaking a spot check, neighbours realising Dawn and I were home alone, someone mentioning two truants to the police: any of these events could have brought our precarious arrangement to an end. What eventually did, however, was the rage building in Dad towards Jose and the fact she had taken Joseph – that and a silly moment of make-believe.

It was one of those bright autumn mornings, perhaps early November 1974. Dad was in between jobs and as we needed to stock up on food he decided to drive us to the shop. He was in a bad mood, perhaps worried about money and having no new work on the horizon. He was also convinced we were being spied on and had become paranoid about it. I used to hear him thinking out loud, muttering, 'That bitch is following me.' Whatever the reason, he was already agitated that day and I was about to make it all a whole lot worse.

Dawn, Frankie and I were in the back seat. Because I wasn't going to school, I was allowed to stay up later than normal, and the night before I had watched *Kojak* on television. In the car, I was in a daydream, thinking about Dad constantly going on about people watching us and wondering what it would be like to be 'tailed', an expression I'd found very funny on the show. Out of nowhere, I said, 'Dad, that blue car behind us, I've seen it outside our house before.'

Dad immediately checked his mirror. There was a blue car. I had noticed it a few moments earlier, but I had never seen it before then.

'Damn! We've got to get back,' Dad said. He swung the car round in a U-turn and we drove home. The blue car passed by and carried on its way.

'Laura, are you sure it's the same car?'

'Yes, Daddy. I think so.' I didn't have the nerve to say I'd made it up.

We arrived home and Dad herded the three of us through the front door and locked it. 'Damn!' he repeated. 'Why can't they leave us alone? Did you see who was in the car, Laura?'

I was all the way into my lie now, too deep to get out. 'I think maybe I saw Jose once,' I told him, making it up. 'Is she going to take Frankie away, Daddy? She loves Frankie much more than she loves me. And she hates Dawn. She was always horrid to Dawn when you weren't here. She doesn't want us, but she might take Frankie. Don't let her, Daddy.' I knew what I was doing was wrong, but it felt like a game, as if it didn't matter if I was making things up, because they weren't true. But it did matter.

Dad was pacing around the room. He was angry and getting angrier. He kept swearing. 'What do you mean that selfish bitch was horrid to Dawn? What did she do? Did she hurt her?' Jose had been mean to Dawn, but I made it sound worse than it actually had been. I wasn't being fair, but Dad had worked himself into such a frenzy that whatever I said was what he wanted to hear. 'She can't treat you like that. She has no right. And she is not taking my boy away from me. Never. I'm going to stop her – stop her now.'

He was in a ferocious temper. I wanted to say that it wasn't true; I knew I should, but I don't think he would have listened even if I had. He marched out, saying, 'Laura, you're in charge. After I leave, lock the door behind me and don't open it for anyone. Not anyone, until I come home.' He never walked through that front door again.

I don't know how much time passed. Hours, I think. We tried to act normal, have something to eat, watch television, but we were upset. I couldn't stop myself repeatedly looking out of the front window, hoping to see Dad draw up in his car. I knew he had set out on a path of destruction and that it was because of me. If only he would come home, everything could go back to normal.

The doorbell rang. We froze. 'Turn the television off, Dawn,' I said, 'and keep quiet.'

'Hello, can you open the door, please? I can hear you in there. Please open the door. This is the police.'

The police! Daddy, I thought, have they come to take me away? Daddy, please come home.

Bang, bang, bang. They were pounding on the door. 'Open up in there. This is the police. Open up, please. You're not in any trouble, but we need to speak to you. Please open the door. It's Laura, isn't it?'

They knew my name. Had Dad sent them? But he'd told us not to open the door to anyone. Not anyone. I didn't know what to do.

A female voice this time: 'Laura, please open the door. We're here to take you to your mummy's. Your father has had an accident and can't look after you. Please let us in.'

A figure appeared at the window. It was dark outside, but I could see it was a policeman. If Daddy was hurt, that made it OK to open the door, didn't it? He hadn't meant for us to keep it closed if he wasn't coming home. Petrified, I stood there, not knowing what to do. Suddenly, the front door flew open, the lock splintering.

There were three police officers, two men and a woman, as well as two other women, social workers. 'Where's my daddy? What have you done with him?' They calmed us down and explained. Your father has been in an accident, they said again. Mum was waiting for us at her flat. They were going to take us there right away. We had to pack our things and be ready in five minutes.

'Is Frankie coming?' I asked. I wanted to bring him with me.

'Don't worry about Frankie, Laura,' said one of the social workers. 'I'll look after him. I'll keep him safe.'

It was a long time before I found out what had happened. In his rage, Dad had gone round to where Jose was living and attacked her. She was very badly injured. He was initially charged with attempted murder, although the charge was later reduced.

Mum was so happy to have Dawn and me home that it softened the blow of the trauma we had been through. As I said earlier, there is nothing like a mother's hug to make you feel better. Mum knew we were back for good now. There was no way Dad could take us away again. He was going to go to prison.

Children adapt quickly. When we had been at Dad's, we had missed Mum, but we'd settled into life there. Now, back in the warmth and stability of Mum's flat, we were happy, but I missed Dad, although I refused to admit it to anyone.

Before the Christmas holidays began, I was in the playground of my new school when one of the girls in my class came up to me. I didn't really know her very well, but her parents were friendly with Mum, who must have been discussing my dad's situation. The girl had clearly overheard the conversation, because I had told no one.

'Your dad won't send you a Christmas present, will he? I know, because he's in prison, isn't he?'

Strangely, I think she was trying to be nice. Maybe she wanted to be my friend. But it made me unhappy and ashamed. I didn't want to speak to her and hated the fact that she knew. I didn't want anyone to know. I made something up and it made me feel better.

'You're so stupid. You don't know anything. My dad isn't in prison. My dad is dead.'

Christmas came and went. We were back in school in Patchway and fell into an easy routine. Summer approached and I overheard Mum and Shaun talking one day. 'The trial finished today, son. Your father was found guilty. He got three years. It'll be on the local news tonight, I think. I don't want the girls seeing it. Make sure you take them out to play.'

Although I didn't fully understand what Mum was saying, I had enough sense not to pester her about it. I could tell this was something very distressing and I was determined not to be the one to make things worse. Later that day, when Shaun suggested we go for a play on the local building site, I grabbed Dawn's hand and made sure she came with us.

That building site was a source of great entertainment for

us. A new development was being built behind our flat and we would spend hours running in and out of the half-built houses, climbing ladders and generally having a ball. Other times, I would be content to sit and watch the men work. I think it reminded me of Dad. It was also a source of inspiration to me.

As the houses grew near completion and the windows were being put in, I noticed the putty they used stayed soft for ages, long after the workmen had gone home. It seemed too good an opportunity to miss. After tea, I would rush down there with an empty bread bag and scrape off a little from around each window and put it in the bag so that it didn't dry out. The next day, I would head off to Rodway Road in Patchway, which was lined with shops. This was long before the invasion of chain stores and mobile-phone outlets. There was a baker, a greengrocer, a newsagent, a wool shop, that sort of thing, and some of them were a bit run-down.

Bold as brass, I would go up to the counter and say in my most grown-up voice, 'Excuse me, I was just passing and I noticed your windows look like they might be leaking. I've got some putty . . . Would you like me to fix them for you?' If I think I have a good idea, or if I've set myself a target, I have never been afraid to give it a go. Sometimes this has landed me in bother, but this character trait has also saved my life.

It never occurred to me that anyone would say no. If their putty was cracked and dried, I could fix that. Incredibly, no one did say no. I must have done at least a dozen shopfronts until the supply of putty dried up (literally).

That summer, we moved house. Mum explained that she was getting divorced from Dad and we were beginning again in a new, three-bedroom house. It wasn't far from the flat and we moved ourselves. The sun was shining as we made repeated trips, carrying bags, laughing, running around. Dawn and I got to choose wallpaper for our room and new bedspreads. I felt very grown up, especially as I was moving into senior school after the summer. It was the happiest and most stable any of us had felt in years. That was a good summer during which, on the back of my putty success, I continued my entrepreneurial endeavours.

Mum has always enjoyed gardening. Even in our little flat we had lots of house plants, and when we moved to the new house we had a tiny back garden. It was heaven and the first thing Mum did was to put in a small vegetable plot, planting anything that would come through quickly. Towards the end of the summer, when the vegetables had grown, she used to dig them up, wash them and hang them on the clothesline to dry. This led to another venture. I decided to make a bit of money by going round the neighbours and Mum's friends selling them the ready-to-eat beans, spring onions, lettuce and whatever else Mum had grown. When she found out, she saw the funny side, fortunately, and we all got a treat from the profits of my early steps in the world of business.

It must have been around the beginning of December when Mum spoke to Dawn and me. 'You know your father is in prison?' she said. 'Well, I've received a letter from the man who helps your father, his solicitor, and in it he says your father wants to see you and that the people who decide these things say you have to go. Only once, if you don't like it. Margaret and Dave will take you. I'm not at all happy about this. He shouldn't be asking. Prison isn't a nice place and I don't want you to go, but there's no choice.'

Dad didn't want to see Shaun and Kevin, and I don't think they wanted to see him. But he wanted to see us, which was exciting and scary at the same time.

The visiting room was grey. That's how I remember it. The walls were grey, the floor was grey and so were all the people. Except for the guards. They were in black uniforms. There were tables scattered around the room and when we walked in I saw Dad immediately, sitting alone, looking old and grey.

'Hello, girls,' he said when we walked over and gave him an awkward cuddle and kiss. 'How are you?'

We didn't really speak much after that. Dad talked with Margaret and Dave, and Dawn and I just looked around. I hated it in there. And Daddy no longer smelled like Daddy. The alcohol fumes had gone.

'Will you have Christmas dinner?' I asked suddenly.

'No, honeybunch, not this year. But I'll make sure to have some turkey-paste sandwiches on the day, and I will think of you two.'

That made me cry. It didn't seem fair that we would be having roast turkey at home, in our lovely new house, while Dad would only have a sandwich. We visited only one more time after that; it was too upsetting.

Chapter Five
I Think I'm Dying

I was never the brightest pupil in my school. In fact, academically I was poor. I was always placed in the lowest class, with the naughty kids. I wasn't interested in learning. Mum knew I wasn't doing very well and, although she tried to help by giving me spelling and counting games at Christmas, her attitude was that somehow I would do OK. I might not get any qualifications, but I would find my own way.

I made a lot of friends at school. I was popular, but I always craved more attention, especially when I was bored. For such a long time, there had been excitement and drama in my life – blazing rows between Mum and Dad, escaping to Sonia's, back to Dad's, Mum coming to try to take us home, Dad attacking Jose, the police. It seemed that there was always something going on and as far as I was concerned it invariably centred on me. Then suddenly everything calmed down and no one seemed to be talking about me any more. I made sure that didn't last for long. I wanted a fuss.

At first, it was the usual stuff: messing about in class, being a bit disruptive and playing truant once (which Mum gave me hell for when she found out – I didn't try that again). It was never anything significant, just enough to get me noticed by my classmates and the teachers.

In needlework class, I instigated a strike. I didn't mind the practical side of sewing. Mum had shown me a lot of the different stitches in the past and I quite enjoyed that. It wasn't hard and it could be fun. But the theory – that was boring. I hated it and didn't want to do it. After two lessons of pure bookwork, I'd had enough. I secretly handed round a note to the class that said reading about sewing was a waste of time and we should let the teacher know exactly how we felt. Everyone nodded in agreement.

The teacher left the classroom for a moment and I quickly scrawled a notice in capital letters and left it on her desk: 'WE ARE ON STRIKE!'

When she returned, we were sitting with our pencils down and our arms crossed. She read the piece of paper and asked what on earth was going on. Not a word was said; we had agreed to stay silent. She marched out and fetched the deputy headmaster. He was not amused. He kept trying to find out who was behind it, but no one grassed me up. It didn't change the class, but for a while I was a bit of a hero in the playground. That was all I wanted.

I even started up a band. It was new-wave music, the sort of thing we were listening to around then, like Blondie or the Boomtown Rats. We were too young to be into real punk. I was the lead singer, naturally, and we wrote a song called 'Ladybird'. It wasn't very good, but I didn't care. For me, it was all about being on stage, with people looking at me.

Like a lot of people, I had my first taste of alcohol at around the age of 13. Mum had a drinks cabinet; although she wasn't much of a drinker, she had a good social life back then – coffee mornings, afternoon teas and people round in the evening. The cabinet was full of gin, vodka, sherry and weird stuff friends had brought back from holidays and given to her as presents.

A friend and I decided to raid it when Mum was out. We each got a tumbler from the kitchen and poured in a fair-sized glug from each bottle, topping them up with water. The result smelled vile, but we drank it in one. We were both very sick. It put me off alcohol for a long time – but not for ever, unfortunately.

I spent a great deal of time fantasising, creating situations in my head that I knew would bring my much-craved-for attention. A girl in my school was knocked down and killed. It was horrible, terribly sad. I wasn't there when it happened, but I saw all the ambulances and police appear. Everyone at the school was traumatised. Teachers and pupils were crying. They eventually built a footbridge over the road in the poor girl's memory. I was upset, but part of me also imagined what it would be like to be hit by a car. I didn't want to get hurt badly or killed, but I wondered what it would be like to be injured enough to be taken to hospital, to have people coming to visit me, perhaps even to get on the local news. That was what I wanted. There were times when I would stand at the edge of the road and will myself to step out, but I never did.

I did attempt to break my leg, however. A friend had broken hers by tripping over and she was in a cast for weeks. Everyone signed it and drew funny pictures, and when she hobbled around the corridors at school, people offered to help, opened doors and asked what had happened – just the kind of attention I wanted. I would climb trees and deliberately fall out or stand at the top of a flight of stairs and tumble down. But it never quite worked. The body has a natural defence mechanism; you instinctively reach out to break your fall or you twist in mid-air to cushion your landing. No matter how hard I tried, I couldn't seem to overcome that instinct. I was bitterly disappointed in myself, which only made me more determined.

I was watching *Newsround* and John Craven was talking about a young lad who had been taken seriously ill after eating the berries of a plant called deadly nightshade. It caught my attention. Looking very serious, the presenter was explaining the dangers while a photograph was flashed up on screen as a warning of what to avoid. I was certain I had seen the very same plant in the local woods and the following day, after school, I was off on my hunt. Sure enough, there it was, nestling in the shade of the trees. According to the report, the berries were the most dangerous part, but the whole plant was poisonous. I plucked a handful of leaves and headed home, looking forward to the drama that was undoubtedly about to unfold over my mysterious illness.

Nothing happened. I ate four or five of the leaves and waited to collapse in front of the family. There was no effect whatsoever. Not even a mildly sore tummy. I think it may have been a wild potato plant.

One of my favourite fantasies was running away. I was going to go with a friend. It was all mapped out, just like when I'd planned to escape from Dad's with Dawn. This new scheme was about as practical. We were to sneak off on a Saturday, to give us as much time as possible before anyone noticed we were gone. Our masterstroke was that we were going to go by rowing boat. That was to stop the dogs that they were bound to send after us from picking up our scent.

Everyone would assume we had gone by road, either hitch-hiking or by bus. Or they would think we had been abducted. That would be the best. They would mount a huge search. But I was certain no one would catch us if we rowed across the Severn and camped in a wood in Wales for a week. That would be long enough, I told my friend. We didn't want to be away for any longer; that wasn't the point. It was the miraculous reappearance I was interested in. The news coverage, the helicopters, the appeals by Mum for our safe return, followed by the fanfare when we stumbled cold and tired into the limelight. Bliss. We never carried out the plan, though, thank God, because soon a wonderful opportunity presented itself, one that was too good to pass up.

I was at a friend's house. We were dropping off our schoolbags before heading to the park to hang around for a while. She was inside and I was waiting for her at the end of her garden path, by the main road, when a van pulled up. The driver rolled down his window and asked for directions. I explained to him where he wanted to go and as he was thanking me, my friend came out of her front door.

'So I should be back on the right road in a couple of

minutes,' the man was saying. 'Thanks'. And he drove off. Something clicked inside me. It was the same feeling I'd had in the car with Dad, when I'd said I thought we were being followed. I knew my friend couldn't have caught everything the man had said, not properly.

'Quick, get back inside. Did you hear what he said? He's going to come back in a couple of minutes and take us away.'

I grabbed my startled friend by the arm and we darted through her front door. 'Did you hear him? Did you hear him?' I shouted at her. 'He's going to kidnap us!'

'Oh God, what do we do? I've got to phone Dad!'

Within minutes, there were police cars screeching to a halt outside the house. Uniformed officers, CID, the whole lot. By the time they arrived, I'd convinced my friend that she had heard exactly what I told her she'd heard: the man had threatened to kidnap us.

The police reaction was very serious. I gave a detailed description of the van, together with half the registration number, which I had memorised, and I had to repeat again and again exactly what the man had said. I made all that up. Mum was called and I was taken to the police station to provide a formal statement. I then sat in a room with a police artist and explained exactly what the driver had looked like. Mum was then informed that I had to stay off school for my own safety. It was even better than I'd dared hope.

A couple of days later, the local free paper dropped through our letter box. We had made the news, under the headline 'Kidnap Alert'. I was delighted. There were no names mentioned, but word soon spread. Everybody began calling to check I was OK – school staff, friends, aunts and uncles. The situation had developed perfectly. Then it all began to unravel.

The police traced the man. He told his side of the story, the truth, and when the police found a witness to corroborate that I had been pointing as if giving directions, the fun and attention petered out. The police said they couldn't take any further action as there was no way to prove a crime had been committed. I never once let on that nothing had really happened. I'm not sure if the police believed me in the end, but I was adamant that the driver had threatened us, and Mum certainly thought every word of my story was true. She was worried about me for a long time afterwards.

It was around the same time, when I was 13, that I first took painkillers. Ever since my periods had started, I had bled heavily and suffered terrible pains. Sometimes it was so bad I would have to stay off school for a couple of days. I didn't mind that, but I hated the excruciating cramps that would come on me in waves. I would be in bed or lying on the sofa and I'd have to curl up into a ball, a hot-water bottle clutched to my stomach, until they subsided.

I was in a bad way one day while some of Mum's friends were round for coffee. Mum explained why I wasn't at school and all the ladies sympathised, which I found a bit embarrassing but also enjoyed. Then one of them asked if I had taken anything to help.

'I give her aspirins, but they don't seem to do very much,' Mum explained.

'You should try giving her a couple of these whenever the pain comes on. I take them for my back and they work a treat. They're perfectly safe. I'm sure if you ask her doctor she can get a prescription.' The lady fished out a small plastic bottle from her handbag and poured a few tablets into Mum's hand. 'These are DGs, distalgesics,' she said. 'She should try them. It can't hurt.'

They didn't just work a treat; they worked like magic. The shooting pains disappeared almost instantly, but that wasn't the half of it. The tablets made me feel wonderful, fantastic, invincible, fearless, floating. Nothing I had experienced came near to how I felt on those pills. I was untouchable: brave, funny, smart, quiet, dreamy, everything. I wanted more. I needed more. But I was smart enough not to say to Mum what they did to me, only that the cramps felt a bit easier. We made an appointment with the local GP and in no time at all I had my own supply. Heaven on earth.

I began taking them when I wasn't on my period – not every day but more often than I should have. Before long, I was increasing the stated dose. That had a double benefit. I would get the buzz that I loved, but if I took too many I would be terribly sick – bouts of vomiting that would last for hours. I never told anyone about taking extra pills, though. I didn't want them taken away from me.

Mum fretted horribly when I was sick like that. I would be off school for days, even once the vomiting had passed, as I would pretend to continue feeling awful. Friends would come to visit, Mum would be clucking around me, even my brothers and Dawn would check in to see how I was doing. Everyone cared about me. Perfect.

I can mark out this period in my life in stages. First stage, legitimate period pains and tablets. Second stage, self-induced sickness. Stage three was when I began to have myself admitted to the children's hospital.

I loved it there – not the ward itself but the visitors, the tests, the attention. Even now, the smell of fresh peaches, brought by friends and family, takes me back to that hospital immediately. I came up with an array of illnesses that no one could prove I didn't have. Crippling headaches, stabbing stomach pains and the old favourite, unexplained vomiting. The fuss around me was everything I could want and I began to perfect my act, so much so that I was prescribed even more distalgesics. The cycle that was to haunt me for years to come had begun.

The more often I was admitted, the more worried the medical staff became. Additional tests were introduced, and the more invasive they became, the happier I was. They would put me under general anaesthetic and send a tube with a camera in through my belly-button – a laparoscopy it was called – to see if they could find the source of my problems.

At first, they found nothing, but that didn't bother me in the least. I knew I could play-act for as long as I wanted. After each examination, I would make a miraculous recovery once I was ready to go home. Then, perhaps the fourth time they did it, I had a stroke of luck. Some tiny cysts were growing on my ovaries – nothing serious but it was the excuse I needed. More pain, more tests, more operations and now I apparently had a concrete medical condition. I made the most of it.

I have no idea how often I was in and out of that hospital. Over the course of two years, certainly more than a dozen times, I'd say. I didn't always have an operation or undergo tests; sometimes I was just in for observation or to rehydrate if I had been violently ill. The truth was every visit was avoidable. There was never anything wrong with me. But I couldn't stay away. I needed the attention. I had become addicted.

Stage four. The end of the cycle. I needed a bigger hit. The laparoscopy was all very well, and the attempts to remove my cysts were satisfying, but I felt I needed to move things up a notch. The visits were becoming routine, the concern less acute.

Mum was out having a meal with friends. By then, Kevin had joined the navy and left home. Shaun still lived with us, but he wasn't around and neither was Dawn. Some days before, I had found a medical textbook in the school library. It was basic but sufficient for what I required. I now knew the symptoms and how to create a drama. I had prepared my act. I felt confident and was ready. Mum had pinned up the number of an emergency doctor in the kitchen in case anything bad happened to me. It was about to.

'Doctor, thank God you're there. I can hardly walk. The pain in my tummy . . . it's so bad. I can't touch it. I think I'm dying.'

After I 'managed' to get out my name and address, the doctor asked me about my symptoms. 'Where does it hurt?'

'My stomach.'

'Where exactly?'

This was key. 'Sort of around my belly-button. Down the right side, as well.'

'Does it hurt when you touch it?'

'Yes, and it feels swollen.' Nice touch. That was going to have him very worried.

'Are you hot, Laura? Have you been sick?'

Yes to both, but not too hot; it's hard to manufacture a temperature.

'Don't move. I'm coming straight over.'

He was extremely concerned about the possibility of a burst appendix. When he arrived, he quickly examined me and then performed one last test, which involved me lying flat with my legs outstretched and him rotating my leg and pulling on my ankle. I was wearing pyjamas and as he undertook his assessment I could feel the bottoms slipping down. I was consumed with fear. The doctor was about to see my pants, or even worse. The yelp of panic he heard was more convincing than anything I could have faked.

An ambulance was called. I watched the flashing blue lights come along our road and saw the neighbours come out to see what was going on, as I had hoped they would, while frantic calls were made to find Mum. Before the doctor had shown up, I had taken some pills to make sure I vomited in the hospital. That clinched it. My appendix was coming out. Mum had been tracked down and was on her way. I was assured she would be there when I woke up. As I drifted off under the general, I was a happy girl.

They discovered that my appendix wasn't ruptured, of course, but the symptoms can exhibit themselves nonetheless. That was how the hospital explained it to Mum, after she had been physically sick with worry in the waiting room. It might have been moments away from bursting, they said. That can be life-threatening.

It was time to appear a scared little girl, although, as the flowers and fruit arrived, life felt good. But a seed had been sown that in a few years' time would almost prove fatal to someone I love with all my heart.

It seems crazy now, but, even with all this going on, I still needed more. Life as it was, at Mum's, wasn't enough for me. I wanted everything to be shaken up again. A humdrum existence, even one that involved frequent visits to hospital, didn't satisfy me. I decided I should move back in with Dad. A new school, a new house and living with Dad, where anything could happen, would provide the excitement I needed. I was certain he would jump at the opportunity. He loved me, after all.

Dad had been released from prison after 18 months, some time towards the end of 1976 or early 1977. Mum never talked about him, but we soon heard he was out. To begin with, I had no interest, but after a year I latched on to this idea of going back to live with him. I made contact through his sister Margaret and she arranged for me to meet him after school one day. I was nervous, but that was good. It was exciting. I didn't tell Mum.

He looked a lot better than he had when I'd visited him in prison. He'd put on some weight and the greyness was gone from his skin. In fact, he looked fairly happy, mellow even.

'I want to come and live with you,' I said straight away. 'I hate it at home.' That wasn't true at all. I wasn't unhappy at Mum's, but I thought saying so, giving him the opportunity to get one over on Mum, would clinch it. It didn't work.

'Laura, honey, that's not possible. I'm sorry. It's not the right time now. I'm trying to get back on my feet again. I hate to say it, but you're better off with your mother. But I would love for you and Dawn to come over. Will you do that?

'I didn't tell you I was out because I didn't know if you'd want to see me. After you stopped coming to visit when I was inside, I thought perhaps you hated me. I'm going to apply to the courts for visiting rights. I don't think your mother will be pleased, but if you wanted to come and say hello, you would make me very happy.'

I couldn't understand what he was saying. Had he stopped loving me? I didn't care that he said he wanted us to visit. I just wanted to go home now. 'Do whatever you want,' I said. 'I might come. I don't know.'

Then he handed me a 50p piece. 'Here, a present from your dad.' I turned and walked away. I felt let down. He'd tried to buy my love with 50p. If only he'd known. He didn't have to purchase it. It was his already. I knew that the moment I saw him.

Dad did apply to see Dawn and me. I had to see a social worker and she asked if I felt comfortable visiting him. Dawn had to do the same thing. I said I guessed so, I didn't really mind. In truth, I did want to see him. Then she started to ask what sort of things I liked doing. Apparently, Dad wanted to make our visits as much fun as possible. I think he was trying to make up for lost time. Did I want any particular toys or books or to do some cooking? I said cooking, to keep her happy.

By then, Dad had moved in with a new partner and they had a baby, Liam. The moment I walked through that door and saw him, a gurgling little treasure of about ten months, that was all I needed.

Dawn and I began to see Dad fairly regularly and the visits went well. I'd look after Liam, and Dawn would play, but as the months wore on I began to get bored. Liam grew up fast. In no time, he didn't seem to need my cuddles in the same way. He was more interested in his mother than me. By the following summer, I stopped going. I was changing.

Dawn carried on and that made me jealous as hell. Suddenly, she was Dad's favourite all over again, just like after she'd been born. She would come back with presents. Once it was an incredible toy sweet shop, with all sorts of jars and scales and multicoloured plastic goodies. I deliberately tried to lose various pieces and snap bits off. This upset Dawn and we had a big argument, at which point Mum became exasperated. She was divorced by then, but the spectre of her ex-husband loomed large in our house. 'He's been gone all this time, but he's still causing trouble, still causing uproar.' She was right. On and off for years to come, Dad was the root of much upset in the family, even if he didn't mean to be. When there has been so much hurt and pain, it never disappears entirely.

My school years were coming to an end and I was ready to leave. I was almost sixteen, and, having missed much of the past two school years through 'illness', I had only a handful of qualifications to my name and no idea about a career. It didn't bother me. I had already visualised the next stage of my life.

I wanted to get pregnant. I wanted a baby of my own.

Chapter Six
We Don't Need to Be Out Long

Having a goal to get pregnant and actually achieving it are two entirely different things. When I left school, I was sexually inexperienced. I was popular and had boyfriends, but the closest I had got to sex was a few fumbles in the park or at parties. I had never gone all the way; it had just never seemed the right moment.

I found leaving school difficult. It wasn't my limited qualifications that bothered me; I missed the social scene. One day, we were in one another's pockets, dealing with the same irritations, worrying about the same inconsequential things, laughing at the same jokes, and then, suddenly, my friends and I went our separate ways. I felt as if it had happened overnight. I had been someone at school and now I found myself abandoned. Sure, we kept in touch, but it wasn't the same. Everyone was facing new challenges, forging new bonds. Everyone except me, that is. The glue that had held my friendships together was brittle and I watched it crumble in front of my eyes.

I was living at home, with no money, no job and nothing much to do except visit my friend and her children. I had met Wendy during my last year at school. She was a bit older than me, married with a couple of kids. She lived nearby and for a while she represented everything I wanted to be. To some extent, I idolised her. It was a thrill to look after her kids, especially the little one, who was barely a toddler, and as my school friends melted into the background I increasingly turned to her for company – much to my mum's annoyance.

Mum didn't approve of Wendy's lifestyle. There was always something going on at her house, friends round and parties, and Mum worried about what exactly was happening and whether Wendy was a bad influence on me. These concerns intensified when Wendy split up with her husband and I began spending more time there, babysitting and staying overnight on her sofa.

The reality was more mundane than Mum might have imagined. I enjoyed Wendy's company. Whatever Wendy did, I did. Whatever she wore, I wore. Sometimes we would go out for an evening to the local pub. It wasn't difficult to get served back then, even though I was only 16. If Wendy ordered a lager and lime, I ordered a lager and lime. She was the height of sophistication and I admired her immensely. If she had something, I wanted it as well. We shared a lot – including her boyfriend.

I had known Alan for while. He lived nearby and, although he was a few years older, I had spoken to him at school because he was friendly with my brothers. Wendy's marriage had been going through a difficult patch for a while, and she and Alan had had a fling during that period, so it was no surprise when they hooked up following Wendy's separation. He was often at Wendy's house when I was there.

Wendy had a part-time job on Saturdays and one Friday night I stayed over to be around first thing in the morning to look after the kids. Alan was there and I was sleeping on the sofa as usual. Early in the morning, I heard Wendy leave, but, as the kids were still in bed, I drifted back to sleep. But not for long.

Alan was standing in his boxer shorts, looking out of the front window. 'Wendy's gone, then?'

'Yeah,' I replied, struggling to claw myself awake. 'About ten minutes ago, I think.'

He turned to look at me, snuggled up in my sleeping bag.

'It's freezing in here,' he said. 'I need to warm up. I'm going to climb in with you, if that's OK.'

I didn't say no.

I should have felt awkward with him pressed up against me – he was my friend's boyfriend – but I felt nothing of the sort. I was excited, and when he began to stroke my hair, my face and then down my body, I responded. I rolled over and kissed him. This was going to be it. I knew it and I wanted it.

In a few frantic moments, I struggled out of my T-shirt and wriggled my pants down, he fumbled out of his boxers and we had sex. We hardly said a word to each other. It didn't hurt as much as I had feared and there was very little blood.

After it was over, I felt relief, not guilt. I had enjoyed the experience, but, more than that, it was the biggest step I had taken to achieving what I wanted more than anything else. Could you get pregnant the first time? I didn't know. I didn't know much about sex at all. It was a forbidden subject at home. The birds and the bees were strictly for Mum's garden. I didn't think it was possible, but if it was and I was already pregnant, then that was fine by me.

The kids would be up soon, so we quickly washed and dressed and were sitting in Wendy's kitchen over a cup of tea when they appeared for their breakfast. We didn't say a word to each other about what had happened. I wasn't embarrassed; I just didn't know what to say. It wasn't until Alan made a move to go home that he brought up the subject we had both been avoiding. 'Are you going to tell her?' he asked.

'No. No, I don't think so.' I had betrayed her, but I thought it was a one-off and that there was no reason she should ever find out. It would only hurt her.

'Good. Agreed. I won't say a word to her either.'

He didn't, but he didn't exactly keep the news to himself. A few days later, I was off to Wendy's again, and as I stepped through the front door she pounced.

'You slept with Alan! You little tart! How could you? I trusted you and the moment I turn my back you shag the bloke I'm seeing – still warm from my bed. Bitch!'

'I'm sorry, Wendy. It just happened. I didn't mean it, honestly. It won't happen again, I promise. How . . . how did you find out?'

'How do you think? He's been boasting about his latest conquest to his mates. You're even more stupid than I thought if you're surprised he didn't keep his gob shut.'

My relationship with Wendy was never quite the same after that. She seemed to forgive me quite quickly, but I knew she would never trust me again. I continued to see her, but we weren't as close and my visits became less frequent. Mum was delighted. She wouldn't have been if she'd known why.

Wendy and Alan had a blazing row about his infidelity and it appeared on the surface that they had split up, but they hadn't really. Perhaps they did for a week, but it wasn't long before he was back round there. And for a while, when he wasn't there, he was with me. I had fallen for him. To me, he was something of a father figure, which I felt I needed. He was stable, calm, kind. But I knew he was never going to leave Wendy properly, not at that time. They were good together, but it was a tempestuous relationship, with as many downs as ups. When they were on a downswing, Alan often called and we would meet at mine, when Mum was out, or we would go for a drive. When we had sex, neither of us used contraception. Alan may have assumed I was on the pill, but it was never discussed.

After that first time with Alan, my mind was set on a clear path that would lead all the way to a baby. I decided that to give myself the best chance I had to cleanse my body of toxins. I had already given up faking illnesses. After having my appendix removed, where else could I go with that? Now I had to rid myself of what was verging on an addiction to painkillers. I was still suffering dreadful period pains and the doctor had continued to prescribe DGs. I was using them sparingly, as the supply I'd got from the hospital had dried up, but the release I felt when I did take them had not diminished. However, the thought of giving birth filled me with such euphoria that I knew I could kick my habit. And I did, for a while. As for the relief the tablets gave me from my awful cramps, I reasoned I wouldn't be plagued with them for very much longer, not after I was pregnant.

Unfortunately, the longed-for pregnancy failed to materialise. Sex with Alan was not regular, but it was surely frequent enough for a 16-year-old girl to be blessed with a child. I began to despair. Was there something wrong with me? Were those once welcome cysts an indication of a problem? The more I thought about it, the more upset I became. I felt the Laura Walsh I wanted to be was disappearing in front of my eyes, and as she slipped from view, so did I. No one was paying me enough attention. Life was passing me by and failing to stop and take notice.

The first time I cut myself, it was easy. I took one of Shaun's razor blades and drew it down my upper arm. No one would see it, but I would know the cut was there. It felt good. The pain of the incision made adrenalin pump through my body. The mere existence of the scar, as I walked down the street, spoke to Mum, acted normal, was enough for a short while. Soon, though, I needed something more.

The fourth time I did it, I cut my cheek. Mum came into my room and saw the blood on my pillow. 'My God, Laura, what happened? There's blood everywhere.'

If I told her the truth, the magic would evaporate. I wanted her sympathy, not her concern. I pretended to be groggy. 'Eh, I don't know what you're . . . oh, I see. I must have cut myself in my sleep . . . the jagged edge of this ring. It doesn't hurt too much. I'm sorry about the pillow.'

She fell for it, bathed my cut and decided it was nasty enough that I had to go to A&E to have it checked out. It required stitches, which gave me a huge buzz, but again it didn't last.

I had begun to hang about with a bloke I'd met through Wendy. He was on the periphery of her crowd and I had come across him once or twice in the pub. As Alan and I were not exactly dating, I said yes when he asked if I fancied going for a drink. I'm not entirely sure why, as he was known as 'Fang'. It wasn't ironic. He didn't have the best teeth. He was OK company, but I didn't fancy him. However, it didn't take long for me to discover that he had certain other, rather appealing qualities.

It must have been about the second or third time we went out. He had picked me up in his car and we were planning on going to a local pub.

'Hi, Laura, do you mind if we go back to mine first? I haven't been home yet and I know Grandma will have cooked my tea.' He lived with his grandmother. 'She gets upset if I miss it.'

His grandmother turned out to be a nice woman, but what appealed to me most was the stack of sleeping pills I noticed the moment we walked into her flat. Loads of them. I needed a lift and I was sure these would not be as strong as the DGs. I'll be safe to pop a couple of those, I thought. It won't have any effect on my chances of getting pregnant. When Fang and his grandma were out of the room, I slipped a packet of the pills into my bag.

I took four the next day. They were great. The black cloud that had been following me around for the past few months vaporised. I felt giddy, happy, sunny. No problem was insurmountable. If my on–off relationship with Alan wasn't getting me what I wanted, the solution was clear. Fang very swiftly fell for my charms. I don't think he could believe his luck, and I couldn't believe what I was doing, especially when the pills weren't working their magic. I made sure we visited Grandma often. If more sex might get me pregnant, more sex it would be. I would do what was required to make that happen.

Fang dropped by the wayside after a couple of months, when his grandmother noticed that a number of packets of pills were missing. She locked them away and blamed the theft on her grandson. With one of my main reasons for hanging around gone, we quickly drifted apart. I felt bad about treating him the way I had, purely as a source for pills and sex. It wasn't fair. He didn't deserve to be used like that.

I had managed to accumulate enough sleeping pills to stave off my persistent feelings of worthlessness. I had used Fang, I still wasn't pregnant and Alan seemed to be spending more time with Wendy and less with me. I needed a lift. I needed someone to notice me. That someone came in the shape of a friend of Wendy's whom I had met on a number of occasions in the past and fancied. His name was Dave and he was funny and popular, with a way about him that I found attractive.

He clearly felt the same, because in early 1981 he asked me out. The only problem was, he was married – and he was on-and-off with Wendy. It didn't stop us. He continued to go home to his wife, but whenever possible we would meet up, sometimes at friends' houses, sometimes out for a drive. I was also still seeing Alan occasionally, and Wendy and I soon found ourselves in competition. If she was with Dave, I'd be with Alan and vice versa, until in April Wendy announced she was pregnant with Alan's baby. By the end of that summer, Alan and I were very much off, but Dave and I were on, whenever we could be.

This went on for about a year. Sometimes for weeks on end, because of holidays or his work commitments, it was impossible for Dave and me to meet up, and in those periods I might hook up with other boys, but it was only Dave I was properly interested in. I still wanted to get pregnant but not by just anyone now. Above anything else, I wanted Dave to be the father of my baby. All I could do was hope nature would take its course.

Until that happened, I realised, it was time for me to take some control of my life. I had been drifting for too long, lost and unhappy save for the snatched moments with Dave. I began to apply for jobs. Despite my spectacular failure academically at school, I could type and my English was in better shape than I deserved. In June, I was successful when WH Smith Wholesale took me on in the admin department.

The work was interesting, and there were cliques and gossip and a lot of fun to be had. It was like being back at school and I fitted right in. I used to hang around with the warehouse guys, messing about in the lunch hour, having tea breaks together, which didn't make me popular with the girls in the office.

In August 1982, Mum arranged a wonderful 18th birthday party for me at the local rugby club. Dave couldn't come – it would have been too difficult – but even that didn't spoil my mood. I was queen for the day and that suited me perfectly. Mum bought me a new outfit, a suit, baggy trousers and a little bolero-style jacket, with braces; the outfit was topped off with ribbons in my hair. Any of the members of Bananarama would have thought they were looking in a mirror. I was the centre of attention and I lapped it up. There was only one thing missing, locked away out of my reach. A few months later, I found the key that would open that door – in a bin at work.

Smith's Wholesale supplied newspapers, magazines and books to trade customers. If the books didn't sell, they would be returned and usually pulped. When the returns arrived at the depot, they were thrown into large crates, ready to be processed. If staff members spotted anything of interest, they were perfectly entitled to help themselves. Many of the books were as good as new and around Christmas the bins were a treasure trove of presents.

During lunch in mid-December, I was idly picking through a batch of returns when a book caught my eye. Or, rather, one word on the cover did: 'Pregnancy'. I hurriedly grabbed it, noticing with delight that the full title was *Everything You Need to Know About Pregnancy*, stuffed it inside my jacket before anyone noticed and casually walked away as if nothing had happened.

I found a quiet spot, tucked away out of sight on the mezzanine level, sat on the floor and started to read. The book was a basic guide to having a healthy baby, from start to end. It was the start I was enthralled by, the very start. I knew there were times in a woman's menstrual cycle when she was more and less likely to conceive, but I had always thought that the optimum time was the last couple of days before your period began, and since I had set my sights on getting pregnant I had tried to have sex during that window. Sitting there on the floor tiles in the offices of WH Smith's, I discovered I couldn't have been more wrong.

Not long after that, I did something stupid. In January, I slipped at work. It was purely an accident, no one's fault, but I hit my head against the floor when I landed. There were a couple of witnesses, who, in a slightly hysterical, overblown manner, described how they had seen my skull crack against the wooden flooring with a sickening thud. It hadn't, but they were clearly enjoying the drama of the moment. However, worries of concussion swept through the first-aiders and before I knew what was going on I was in an ambulance and on my way to hospital for a thorough check-up.

I liked lying in the ambulance with my head bandaged and the crew fussing over me. I had forgotten the feeling. I can milk this for a few days, I thought. They'll never know.

That was how it started. To begin with, it was all about enjoying the attention once again. But it soon got out of control. I told the hospital staff that I couldn't see out of my left eye. Alarm bells started ringing. Optical nerve damage, detached retina, all sorts of possibilities were tested for, but nothing was found to be wrong – because there was nothing wrong. The only problem was that I was stuck with the lie for years. It's hard to remember over such a long period which eye you're not meant to be able to see out of.

Smith's feared a compensation claim and the moment I got wind of that I contacted a solicitor who specialised in such matters and he agreed to take me on. By this stage,

Smith's had sent me to various specialists, none of whom could find any damage. Having become convinced I was pulling a fast one, they decided to refer me to one of the country's top eye surgeons for an assessment. He was too clever for me. He placed a pair of glasses on me, the type that allows the doctor to cover each eye separately. This was nothing new to me.

'Now, Miss Walsh, I want to test the reflexes in your good eye. I'm going to quickly cover and uncover your right eye. Each time you can see, I want to you to tell me which letter my colleague is holding up.'

He stood behind me and raised and lowered the slide over my right eye, leaving my left eye, my 'bad' one, open.

Open: 'B'. Closed: don't say anything. Open: 'X'. Open: 'C'. Closed: keep quiet. Still closed: keep quiet. Open: 'T'. Open: 'G'. Open: 'W'. Closed: 'K'.

Damn. My right eye had remained covered, but I had read the card. They knew. But I wasn't giving in.

We found one expert who said that if someone believes they have suffered a serious injury, then it is effectively as bad as if it had actually happened. That became the basis for the claim. I wish we had never come across that person. I wish I had admitted defeat in the specialist's room, gone home, gone to sleep and woken up with the joyous and incredible news that my sight had returned and that any claim for compensation was to be forgotten in celebration of the miracle.

But I didn't. I pushed it and pushed it, determined to lay my hands on a pot of gold that inevitably remained out of reach. Eventually, after four years, I agreed to drop my case. I was worn down by it; I wasn't going to win and I didn't deserve to. And by then a tragedy had struck that made such pointless scams seem pathetic and worthless – for a time, anyway.

Within a couple of weeks of the accident, I insisted on returning to work to undertake tasks suitable for a secretary whose sight is severely restricted. I thought it would strengthen my claim if I was seen to be trying to overcome my 'disability'. I was being so brave. Besides, I also knew that I was not going to be there for very much longer, not if I could put my plan into action.

It was the second week of February 1983. Dave rang to see when we could meet that week. 'Why not tonight?' I suggested.

'I was thinking more the end of the week because . . .'

'I'd really love to see you tonight, Dave. Please. I miss you. We don't need to be out long.'

He agreed. We stayed out long enough. By the time I got home, I was sure I was pregnant.

Chapter Seven
Make This Stop

I decided not to tell Mum I was pregnant, not until I was well past the point of no return. I learned when that was from my pregnancy book. I knew that, after she'd recovered from the shock of her virgin daughter carrying a child (she had no idea that I had ever slept with anyone), Mum would insist that I have an abortion if I told her any earlier.

I delayed telling her, or anyone, for as long as possible. The office was being refurbished and if the girls at work had been more aware they might have noticed that the smell of paint made me rush repeatedly to the toilets in the morning. I didn't have a boyfriend as such, so I guess no one was really considering the possibility that I might be pregnant.

I suspect my great-aunt knew, though. I used to spend a lot of time with her, and one day while I was at her house one of my teeth snapped off when I was eating a satsuma. She rushed me to the dental hospital, where I was attended to. The nurse on duty asked if I was pregnant, explaining that weakened teeth can be an indication. I denied I was and the breakage was put down to a lack of calcium in my diet, but, from the look in her eyes, my great-aunt thought differently. She didn't say a word to anyone, God bless her.

I was lucky that I didn't show, not for the first four months, anyway. During that period, I acted normally, squeezing into my tight jeans and dancing the night away to 'Billie Jean' and the rest of the hits of 1983 at the local disco. By month five, there was a bump, but baggy tops made it easy to hide.

It was hard not telling anyone. This was what I had dreamed of for years. I was going to be a mother, with a new life to look after; I wanted to shout it from the rooftops. On the other hand, keeping it secret made me feel important. I liked that. I knew something that no one else did, not even Dave.

On Saturdays, I would take the bus into town to wander around Mothercare and the new-baby sections in department stores, imagining my child in the clothes I picked up or looking up at me from the various prams on display. In John Lewis, I saw the most beautiful crib imaginable. It was round and white, with a cover and bedding of gorgeous embroidered cotton. It was expensive, but my heart was set on it. The fact that I couldn't buy anything didn't matter. I was content in my own world, the one I had created for myself.

The dreaded day couldn't be put off for ever. Mum had to be told eventually. I was living in her house, for goodness' sake. She was bound to realise something was up very soon. I tried to picture the scene. Making her a cup of tea, sitting her down in our lounge: 'Mum, I've got something to tell you. I know this will be a shock, but I'm very happy. I'm having a baby.' There is a moment of silence before Mum bursts into tears. She is horrified. She starts saying how I have brought shame on her and the family, how I have let them down, how she can never face her friends again. Just thinking of it made me feel sick inside. I couldn't do it. I asked Wendy.

Wendy was incredible. Her baby with Alan was about 18 months old, but the relationship wasn't going well. The first thing she said to me when I told her was, 'Is it Alan's or Dave's?' She knew about Dave and me. I told her that I wasn't going to say who the father was and that he didn't even know himself. She accepted that and didn't judge.

'Does your mum know?'

'No. I don't know how to tell her. I don't have the guts. Would you do it for me?'

'I'll do it tonight,' she said. There was no going back now.

I was at Sonia's when Mum called. 'Get back here now.'

Wendy left when I arrived and the scene was almost word for word as I had imagined: tears, recriminations, accusations.

'How could you do this to me? Wait until your father hears about this. He's going to think I'm the biggest slag on earth, bringing up an unmarried teenage mother.'

Dawn was shocked and Shaun showed little reaction, but Kevin was angry when I called to tell him. He liked everything to be done by the book and in his eyes this most certainly was not the right way of going about things. We had a huge row about it when he was next home. I had no option but to sit through these differing reactions. It was upsetting, but nothing anyone said made me regret what had happened.

Now that it was out in the open, I could go shopping. The first thing I brought back was a pair of white woollen booties. I didn't know if I was having a boy or a girl, so I deliberately chose neutral colours. The ice in Mum's heart began to melt. Next, I brought home a tiny babygro and a bobble hat, and that was it. Baby fever engulfed us. We were all excited about the new arrival, even Shaun. We started making plans for a nursery, talked endlessly about names and imagined what he or she might become when they were older. I loved every second of it.

Questions were asked about the father. There was a lot of pressure, talk of financial responsibility, that sort of thing. I wasn't interested, but to keep the peace I gave the impression that the dad was an ex-boyfriend whom I'd only gone out with for a short time and whom I no longer saw and that he didn't want anything to do with it. My family were not pleased, but it kept the constant questioning at bay.

I told Dave the truth. He was happy for me, but he was married and his wife was expecting. I didn't want anything from him and he didn't offer. I promised I would keep his identity a secret and would raise the baby on my own, although inside I wanted more. When I closed my eyes and imagined my happy family, Dave was there, but I knew I couldn't pressure him. We were still seeing each other during this period and I decided to wait and see what happened. Anyway, something far more important was taking up my attention: having the baby.

I grew huge in month six and had to leave work. What with my 'injured' eye, I hadn't been doing much typing and secretarial work, which had meant taking on more physical activities, including lifting. That quickly became impossible, and I left a good two months earlier than I might have done otherwise.

I was desperate to get the baby out. It was my main focus. I'd never smoked and I'd stopped going to the pub and had given up the sleeping tablets. I didn't need anything to give me a buzz; I was on a permanent high. I just wanted to hold my baby and I became increasingly impatient to do so.

Sitting in the bathroom at home, I looked at the knitting needle in my hand. It was Guy Fawkes Night and moments before I had been looking out of my bedroom window as fireworks lit up the early-evening sky. The thought had burst into my mind: what a lovely night to give birth, the perfect birthday for my child. I was due within a week, but if I could break my waters now, by midnight I would be holding my baby. All I needed to do was insert the knitting needle gently, prick myself and it would all start. I sat back, lifted my legs and pushed it in. I was so, so careful. No jerky movements, no stabbing.

Then I thought, what am I doing? This is crazy. I could damage my baby. I can't force nature. If only I had remembered those thoughts 18 months later. In frustration, I let the knitting needle fall to the floor. I wanted my baby now, but there was no way to make that happen.

I had been feeling unwell, dizzy and tired. I went into hospital for some tests and it was discovered that my red-blood-cell count was low. I was anaemic – not dangerously so but they wanted to monitor me regularly. Four days after my due date, I was asked to come in for an internal examination. The blood coating the nurse's gloved hand caused considerable concern. The placenta was lying low and it was decided that I should be induced. I was delighted. It meant I knew exactly when my baby was going to be born.

My waters were broken and I was hooked up to a drip to speed up the contractions. Mum had accompanied me to the hospital. As we waited in the delivery room, a television was showing a Saturday evening variety show on which Lionel Richie was performing his recent single 'All Night Long'. Mum smiled across at me. 'How appropriate,' she said. She was wrong.

The monitors began to indicate the baby's heartbeat dropping. I am a small woman and the worry was that if I gave birth naturally it might stress the baby to such an extent that the dropping heartbeat could be dangerous. I required an immediate Caesarean, under general anaesthetic.

The first thing I saw when I woke was the top of my daughter's head. I knew it was a girl instantly. Her dark hair was poking out from a blanket in the cot next to my bed. She had been asleep, but she woke the moment I did. She looked up at me. I had spent years imagining this moment. My wildest fantasies didn't come near to the truth. When those beautiful eyes turned to me, the whole world stopped. I couldn't move. I didn't want to. All I cared about was looking at this beautiful creature that I had created. Nothing else mattered apart from her. I could feel the tears trickling down my cheeks, but still I didn't move. I loved this little girl more than life itself.

The world began to turn again. A nurse came in and gently lifted my girl into my arms. That first touch of her skin. Her first breath on my face. We were connected for all time. I knew that. My life was never going to be empty again. I would never be lost with her next to me. She was so soft, so pretty, and when she smiled at me, her mum, I vowed to myself that I would protect her for ever. Nothing would harm this little girl, I would see to that. She would want for nothing. I would always be there for her, no matter what. I would never let her suffer the dreadful consequences that alcohol and violence inflict on a family. Over the next 27 years, I didn't manage to keep all the promises I made that night, but I never forgot them.

Karissa. That's what I called her. I was allowed to take her home after a week. Waiting for her was the love of a family, toys, teddy bears, mobiles hanging from the ceiling and the wonderful crib from John Lewis. Mum had bought it for her. Lying in it, she looked as though she was a gift from heaven.

We stayed at Mum's for about eight months and in that time it seemed to me I hardly held Karissa. If it wasn't Dawn who had her, it was Mum, Sonia, Wendy or Shaun, or even Kevin when he was home on leave. He became swept away in the joy and excitement. It was a wonderful time. Karissa slept through the night and laughed through the day.

When Dave saw his daughter, I could tell he loved her dearly. His eyes shone in a way that I had never seen before. His wife had had her baby a few months earlier, but their relationship was all but over. Both of them accepted that. After Karissa was born, Dave and I continued to see each other, secretly still. Then, when I applied for and was granted a little flat opposite Mum's, Dave came round to help me decorate and move in, and he never left. We explained the truth to Mum and she gave us her blessing. I was happy.

Life settled into a relatively comfortable pattern. Dave was working during the week, but with Mum and Dawn living opposite I had a lot of support as I learned to be a mum. I found it hard, but I was coping. At the weekends, Dave and I would socialise with our friends while Mum did the babysitting. We'd go to the local Legion club. Strong lager and blackcurrant became my drink of choice and I began to look forward to the release it gave me after a week with my baby. Sometimes I would end the evening quite drunk; we all would. It was social and fun, nothing more, but I had taken the first steps down a destructive road. As Dave and I laughed and joked our way through that first year together, I could never have imagined where it would lead.

Dave's divorce was proceeding and he had no contact with his wife or their child. I think they both realised that a complete break was better for everyone involved. It certainly made my life easier. My thoughts turned to completing my dream life with another baby. Not any baby: a baby boy.

Just over a year after Karissa was born, I became pregnant again. Ideally, though, it would have happened a couple of months earlier or later. I had decided that a summer baby meant a girl and I wanted a boy. Husband, wife, girl, boy: that's how I planned it and that was how it was going to be – no matter what.

I can only try to explain why I felt my baby had to be born before or after certain dates; I know it makes no real sense. I had created a fantasy, and if things didn't happen the way I'd imagined them, everything would be ruined. That was how I saw life. As I had to have that teddy bear, so I had to have a son. And, as far as I was concerned, that meant giving birth no later than the end of June. As winter moved into spring and the days grew longer, the strength of my conviction increased to a certainty, but I kept it to myself. I was due on 13 August, three days before my birthday, four before Dawn's. That was when girls were born.

It's lunchtime on 29 June 1985. I am knocking on the door of an older couple opposite, Beryl and Phil. We know them well and have spent time in their flat. On one of those evenings, I noticed a bottle of pills in the kitchen. DGs, the ones I used to take for my period pains. The tablets registered in my subconscious, but I didn't think about them until this morning. I had no reason to before then, but I woke up in a panic and remembered the invincible feeling they used to give me. Only two days left in June. I have to do something, but I need a boost before I do. As I knock on the door, I am stooped over.

'Beryl, I'm glad I caught you. I know it's really cheeky of me, but I hope you can help.'

'Of course, Laura, anything. What's wrong? Is it the baby?'

'No, nothing like that, don't worry. It's my back. I couldn't sleep a wink last night and this morning I can hardly bend to dress Karissa, let alone pick her up. I've taken some paracetamol, but they've had no effect at all. Then I remembered you mentioning that Phil sometimes has a bad shoulder and he got something from the doctor that really helped. I'm going to make an appointment at the surgery, but I don't think I can make it down there like this. Do you have anything that could see me through?'

'Of course. Hold on, I'll fetch them. Can I help with Karissa or anything? Do you need a lift?'

'Thanks, Beryl. If the pills don't work, I'll let you know.' I know they will work.

Late afternoon. Dave is opening the passenger door of his car, helping me out. We are outside the hospital. He thinks I have gone into labour. I haven't.

'It's all right, Lor, it's all right. You're going to be fine.' He's worried. He knows I'm not due for another six weeks. 'You and the baby are going to be fine. We're here now. The doctors will look after you. It's going to be OK.' I know it is. The pills have reassured me.

What an act I put on. Even though my waters haven't broken, everyone in the room – doctors, nurses, the midwife – thinks I am going into labour. They're trying to do all they can to stabilise me in the hope that the contractions will pass and the baby won't arrive today. Everyone hopes that – except me.

They have strapped some sensors to my belly, to monitor the contractions. There aren't any, of course, but when I secretly push down on them with the palms of my hands, the machine registers, as I hoped it would. I am not dilated, but that doesn't cause any suspicion. I wasn't dilated when I had Karissa either. The X-rays they took then indicated that because of my small frame my cervix wouldn't open. I could never have given birth naturally. It was always going to be a Caesarean.

I start to scream as if I'm in pain. 'For God's sake, help! I can't take it any more. I feel like I'm being stabbed. Please give me something to take the pain away. Make this stop.' I haven't mentioned the distalgesics I took only a few hours previously, and I took more than I should have.

They give me a pethidine injection, which, on top of what I have already taken, makes me violently sick. As I throw up for the fourth or fifth time, I can sense the rising panic in the room. This latest development seems to have tipped the balance in my favour. I can hear hurried conversations. I am beginning to feel genuinely ill – tired, confused and dehydrated. I am hooked up to a drip and beginning to look dreadful. The colour has drained from my face. The decision is taken to operate. There appears to be no other option. They are running the risk of losing the baby, it seems.

As dreadful as I feel, just before the anaesthetic knocks me out, I look at the clock on the wall. It is 2.30 a.m. on 30 June. I am going to have a boy.

Ricky weighed just over five pounds when he was born, six weeks early and very poorly. When I came round, he wasn't lying in a cot next to me as Karissa had been; he was in the special care unit. He was having difficulty breathing because his lungs weren't properly formed. Not unusual in premature babies, I was reassured. He was in the best possible place and he was fighting. All the signs were good. They gave me a Polaroid snapshot of a tiny bundle. My son. I wouldn't hold him for another 24 hours.

I should have been horrified by what I had done, but I wasn't. I was calm. I had my son. Life was complete. The Laura Walsh story was coming out exactly as I had planned.

Ricky remained in hospital for most of the summer, undergoing constant tests, with round-the-clock monitoring. It was a long time before he could breathe without assistance, and he wasn't putting on the weight he should have been. My little boy was so fragile, because of me, and had very few resources to fight off infections. But he was tough and after nine weeks I was allowed to bring him home.

Within a fortnight, he was back in hospital. He'd woken up in the night clearly in distress, struggling to breathe, turning blue. Dave stayed with Karissa, and I rushed Ricky to A&E in a taxi. He had pneumonia and was taken away from me for immediate treatment.

The next time I saw him, it was one of the worst sights I have ever seen. He was back in the special care unit, curled in a ball, tubes protruding from his little arms and tiny head, and he was screaming as if in agony. I thought my stupidity was going to kill my son. The doctors explained that they were worried he had brain damage because of this early birth and that they had performed a lumbar puncture to draw fluid in order to ascertain the level, if any, of the damage. He was suffering horrendously and I had caused it.

Somehow, Ricky survived. His will to live was strong. I was incredibly proud of my little boy. I still am. The tests he'd endured came back negative and he responded to the medication he was given for the pneumonia. After a further two weeks in the hospital, he came home again. It was explained that because he was frail any germs he might pick up could be more dangerous than they normally would be. We were advised to keep a constant eye on him and to bring him in if there was ever anything wrong. Over the next six months, he was in and out of hospital until he began to put on weight and build up his defences.

We had been given a heart monitor when Ricky had first come home from the hospital, and we attached it to his chest every night. If he stopped breathing, an alarm would sound and we had detailed instructions on how to resuscitate him if necessary.

The flat we lived in was cramped enough with the four of us, and in October that year it became a lot more crowded.

Ricky was not long home after his battle with pneumonia when my brother Shaun called to say he had nowhere to stay. He'd had a huge argument with Mum and she'd told him to get out.

'There's a bed for you here, Shaun, you know that. Always.'

'But your place is tiny, Laura. There's no room.'

'We'll make room. You're family. We'll work it out.'

Shaun was right, there wasn't really enough room, but there was no other option. It would take him a while to find a place of his own. Dave understood and Shaun moved into Karissa's room. She slept on a little folding Z-bed in our room, next to her brother. It was far from ideal, but we coped as best we could.

One benefit of Shaun staying was that we suddenly had a live-in babysitter and we took full advantage. It was good to be out of the flat, and although I was probably overdoing it with the drink, I never felt it was a problem or that I should be at home with the kids every night. Shaun had the number for the Legion and we were less than five minutes away should there be a problem. We had explained about Ricky's heart monitor and Shaun understood what he had to do. We were having a good time. Everything seemed to be on the up. However, there always seemed to be one more thing I felt was needed to complete the picture. This time it was a house.

Shaun's arrival had confirmed to me that we needed a new place to live. The flat had meant the world to me when Dave and I had first moved in, but we had outgrown it. I wanted more space and a garden. That was what happy families had. We applied to be rehoused and started looking. In early December, we found a place we liked, and at the same time Shaun secured a flat for himself. It had to be a good omen. Both places were going to be available the following March.

That Christmas was a joy. We were packed into our flat like sardines and it was exhausting looking after two children, but it didn't matter. We could see the future and it was what we wanted. We were happier than any parents had ever been: safe, secure, in love, with a common purpose to make things even better. Dave, me, a double buggy and a new house on the horizon. Perfect.

Then, in February, I discovered I was pregnant again.

Chapter Eight
Time to Wake Up

Having a coil fitted had seemed to be the perfect solution. Dave and I were in a loving relationship, but I had been wary of going on the pill. I was sufficiently self-aware to realise I wasn't disciplined enough to remember to take it every day, especially when I was looking after two children. Fully alert, it was unlikely; in a state of almost total exhaustion, there was no hope.

Unlike his sister, Ricky was a dreadful sleeper, possibly as a consequence of how he'd arrived in the world. He never slept through the night and during the day it was impossible for me to snatch even the shortest of naps. It seemed the only time Ricky wasn't crying was when I fed him a bottle, picked him up or took him out in the buggy for a walk. Then there were the constant visits to the doctor. If it wasn't a cough, it was a painful ear infection or a dreadful cold. In my heart, I knew I was responsible, but it didn't make things any easier to cope with. I couldn't drive and Dave was out all day. I loved both my children dearly – they were everything I had ever wanted – but at the same time I found myself at the end of my tether trying to hold it all together.

If I wasn't going to go on the pill, then the coil was the safest option. There was one cast-iron certainty that dominated the situation: I didn't want another child. The thought of trying to look after three petrified me. I was on the edge with two; a third would be impossible.

Almost from the day the coil was fitted, it didn't feel right.

Initially, I put it down to the expected discomfort that I had been warned I might experience for the first couple of weeks. However, that stretched into months with no improvement and evolved into soreness. Sex became out of the question. The coil was in the way. To make matters worse, I was also bleeding a lot more than I should have been, throughout the month.

I ignored these problems, however, putting them down to having the coil fitted so soon after giving birth to Ricky and the fact that I'd had both children by Caesarean. I supposed that my small frame, coupled with the fact that I hadn't ever given birth naturally, meant my body was taking time to adjust to the device. Until it began to slip out.

I was out walking with the kids when I first felt it move. It was towards the end of February and frost still coated the cars parked next to me. I stopped, in a panic, and could feel a trickle of blood running down my leg. More than a trickle. And the soreness had moved on a stage. I was in real pain.

I made it back to the flat and examining myself in the bathroom I felt the hard end of the coil with my fingertips. It was almost out. I couldn't see how I could make it to the doctor's in the state I was in. I knew I shouldn't do it – I was aware it was a risk – but a gentle tug on the strings attached to the coil was surely all that was required. But it was stuck. There was no alternative: I pulled on the longest coat I had and shuffled up to the surgery, fearful that a red line would be marking my route. The doctor knew exactly what was required and in a matter of seconds the coil was out. The relief was immense.

Call it a mother's instinct, call it fear, but within days of the coil being removed I knew I was pregnant. A return to the doctor confirmed what I was already sure of. The only surprise was how far along I was: almost 16 weeks.

I was distraught. Back home, the tears that had welled up at the doctor's came in a flood. The thought of another child was too much to deal with. The baby was due at the beginning of August. I would be a twenty-one-year-old mother of three kids under three. Ricky needed so much looking after, constant attention. Karissa was growing up fast and I wanted to be with her for every new step she took. I had Dave, I had a daughter and a son, we were moving to a new house. I had what I'd set out to have. This was going to ruin everything. How could I bond with another child? How could I love another child? I would have no time or energy. It was unfair. I had taken precautions. I hadn't been reckless, but my body had let me down. I didn't deserve this. There was nothing I could do, except cry.

Dave tried to reassure me that everything would be OK. I wasn't to worry. He'd make sure we had enough money; he'd make our new home exactly how I wanted it. It would all work out. 'Trust me, Lor, we'll cope.'

We moved three weeks later. By then, I had come to terms with my pregnancy. I was excited about our new house, which helped, even though it required a lot of work. It was what we wanted: a three-bedroom house in a good location. Perhaps best of all, from my point of view, it was around the corner from an old friend, Annette. I had first met her when I was 13. She'd lived across from Mum's flat and at the time she had a two year old, Simone, whom I used to take out for walks. Annette and I became close and I was upset when she moved after having her second child. We lost touch for a few years and I was thrilled when I discovered we were to be neighbours once again.

Dave and I put in to buy the new house immediately. An old lady had been living there for a number of years and hadn't undertaken any modernisation, but in many ways that wasn't a bad thing. It meant we could start from scratch. The only major problem was that it was cold. There was no central heating and that was going to be expensive to install. We would need to save for that over a number of months, but in the meantime we had plenty to keep us occupied.

We decorated the kids' rooms first. My Little Pony for Karissa,

Thomas the Tank Engine for Ricky. We decided he was strong enough now to be on his own. The new arrival would sleep in our room. Dave worked incredibly hard to make the place homely as quickly as possible. I used to look at my man working away and smile. Dave had been right; we were coping. As summer grew nearer, I became excited about our new baby. Life was hard and I was still living in a fog of tiredness, but I hadn't collapsed, the pregnancy was relatively plain sailing, the purchase was going through and the house was taking shape. After the decorating, Dave turned his attention to the kitchen, fitting new units and laying Flotex flooring. It was stain-resistant, clean and warm, and I could imagine three children crawling around on it in our happy home.

When I went in for my Caesarean on 1 August 1986, I was as excited as I had been with both Karissa and Ricky. I was sure it was going to be a girl. It was a summer baby, after all. When I picked Natasha up for the first time that evening, more than seven pounds of healthy, noisy baby, even the most remote of lingering doubts took flight. She was beautiful and I loved her. I would manage no matter what. She needed me and I would be there for her.

I made certain there would be no more, though. The hospital resisted at first – I was not yet 22 – but I was adamant. I wanted to be sterilised. I wanted my tubes cut, not merely tied. There would be no more births after this one. As Natasha was pulled from my womb, the incisions were made. My smiling, gurgling baby girl would be my last child.

The six days Natasha and I spent in hospital together were bliss. Why had I ever worried about bonding with her? She was adorable, perfect in every way. The family visited, Karissa was obsessed with her little sister and I was given the opportunity to sleep as much as I could. I arrived home feeling as if nothing could stop me and my family now. We weren't quite the Waltons, but we were set fair for happiness.

It didn't last long. The reality hit me within days. My recuperation in hospital felt like a lifetime ago. Everyone needed something from me all the time. It was constant and the tiredness I felt was brutal. Natasha would need to be fed and changed, Ricky would start crying, then Karissa would be hungry. Or Ricky would be running a temperature and it was off to the doctor. At night, Natasha, lying in the cot next to our bed, would make noises in her sleep, keeping herself company in the darkness of the night, keeping me awake. And if she didn't banish sleep, Ricky did. He would wake at least once in the night, requiring a change and a bottle. Karissa, thank God, slept through it all.

If it hadn't been for Annette, I would not have been able to cope at all. She was a source of advice, companionship and support. She had four children by this time and we spent a lot of time together, round at her house or taking the kids for a walk. Having her near gave me a sense of security, but she couldn't be there every moment I needed her. Mum and Dawn did all they could to help, but they both had jobs and Dawn now had a separate life of her own, living with her boyfriend.

I stumbled on, overwhelmed much of the time. The anchor of my perfect family life was almost imperceptibly beginning to work itself loose. Occasionally, I felt the shift, but I ignored it, telling myself that every day the children grew older was a day nearer the sanctuary of routine, sleep and taking control of my life again.

Karissa starting nursery a couple of months after Natasha was born should have been a blessing, a respite from the constant demands of three children, but the organisation required in taking her, picking her up and being on call should she need me during the day actually added to my escalating anxiety. There were just too many things to think about, too much to organise and I never had a moment to myself. I began to feel crushed. As I struggled to survive each day, the tension in the house rose and the rows between Dave and me intensified.

For once, Ricky was sound asleep in his cot. He'd been up

early, I'd fed him and he'd gone back to sleep. Karissa's coat was on, ready to go to nursery. Natasha was in the buggy. I put my hand on Ricky's head and was about to stroke him back to consciousness when I hesitated. He looked peaceful, deep in his dreams. If I wake him now, I thought, he'll cry and wriggle and scream his way along the road. It's only ten minutes. No one will know, he'll stay asleep. It would be wrong to wake him, not fair. The best thing to do is to leave him here. For his own sake. You're doing it for him, Laura.

I was barely out of the house when Dave pulled up. 'I forgot my wallet. I'm going back to pick it up now. Did you persuade Annette to take Ricky?'

There was no way I could lie. Dave always had a special place in his heart for Ricky, partly because of how ill he had been when he was born and how hard he had fought.

The anger and frustration that had been building between us over the past few weeks was there, there was no doubt, when I told him no one was looking after his boy. But it was controlled, as though he couldn't quite believe it. 'You've done what? You've left our son on his own? What if he wakes up? What if he coughs and chokes or climbs out of his cot? What's wrong with you? Have you gone fucking mental?'

When I got back to the house with Natasha, Dave was there. He'd calmed down and Ricky was fine. 'Lor, you need some help,' he said. 'I know this must be hard. Talk to the health visitor when she comes round next. And could you find someone to take Natasha for the odd night? Lynne perhaps? You need to do something.'

We'd met Lynne when we'd first moved into our flat. She had a couple of kids who were a bit older, and she loved babies. When I asked, she was more than happy to help with Natasha. I also spoke to the health visitor on her next visit. Previously, I had tried to hide the level of stress I had been feeling. I didn't want to seem like a failure. It felt good to open up. 'I don't think I can carry on any longer,' I told her. 'It's too much.'

Home help was arranged and slowly the pieces began to fall into place. When Natasha was at Lynne's for the night, I at least got some sleep, and the home help made sure the house was clean and tidy and there was food in. It wasn't that I hadn't been managing to do those things, but not having to think about them every day when I was struggling to function with tiredness lifted the pressure and allowed me some freedom to breathe. Almost overnight, a corner had been turned.

Despite all the renovations and decorating we had undertaken on the house, it remained cold. The original storage heaters were old and ineffective. The new central-heating system became a priority and by the beginning of December we had saved enough. The work was going to be disruptive for a few days and Lynne kindly offered to look after Natasha for me. Dave and I decided to take advantage of this window of opportunity to rearrange the bedrooms in the hope that if Natasha was no longer sleeping in the cot next to us, we might manage a couple more hours' sleep a night. Dave and I agreed that that would be the best Christmas present we could give each other. We discussed the various permutations at length.

As Ricky was still waking up for a bottle most nights, he might disturb Natasha if she slept in his room. Equally, Natasha might wake Karissa if they shared. We decided in the end that the best option was for Ricky and Karissa to take the bigger room at the top of the stairs and for Natasha to sleep in the small room next to ours. We would hear her instantly if she woke and started to cry.

When Lynne brought Natasha back after two nights away, I was excited. I had missed her terribly; we all had. The smile she gave me first thing in the morning, the beautiful contented way her lashes would flutter when she was feeding, the way her eyes followed her sister and brother around the room, whatever they were doing. For all that I had been devastated when I'd discovered I was pregnant, she was a much-loved member of the family. We fitted together.

The work had gone well, the house was beautifully warm and the rearrangement of the beds had been painless. Ricky and Karissa had shared for the past two nights and hadn't disturbed each other, even when Ricky woke for his bottle.

Once Karissa and Ricky had gone off to bed, I gave Natasha a bath and decided to feed her a bit later, in the hope that this might help her sleep through the night. Dave and I then sat up for a couple of hours, watching television and making a list of presents for the kids. It was a very ordinary, happy, normal evening.

We went to bed around midnight. Ricky woke around 3 a.m. and I gave him his bottle. I was on automatic pilot and once he was settled again I fell straight back to sleep. Everything was peaceful in the house; it was lovely and warm, content.

Radio 1 woke me at seven o'clock. I lay dozing for ten minutes as Dave got ready for work. He made himself a cup of tea and a slice of toast, kissed me goodbye and was off. I could hear Karissa and Ricky beginning to stir in their room. It was time to be up. As I pulled on my dressing gown, I congratulated myself on how well feeding Natasha that little bit later and letting her sleep in her own room had worked. She hadn't stirred in the night and was still asleep. I decided to leave her while I saw to the other two.

When I next noticed the clock, it read 8.30. Karissa and Ricky were washed and dressed and ready for breakfast. It was time Natasha was up. She loved breakfast time, watching the other two. And anyway we had to leave in 45 minutes to take Karissa to nursery. If Natasha has suddenly reached the stage of sleeping through the night, I thought as I climbed the stairs, life is going to be a lot easier from now on.

The heat hit me the moment I opened her door. Natasha's room felt like a sauna. It was a small room, the heating had been on all night, low, and we hadn't left a window open because it was cold outside.

She was making little hiccup noises in her cot. I had never

heard her doing that before. It didn't sound right. Something was wrong with my baby girl. Very wrong.

I leaned over to pick her up. 'Time to wake up. Mummy's here.'

Her cheeks were flushed, her eyes shut. As I took her in my hands, she was limp, her legs dangling, her head lolling. Still her eyes were closed, but she continued to make those little noises. She's just too hot, I tried to reassure myself. She'll be fine in a moment. But my heart was telling me something different. As I held her to me, I couldn't feel the little puffs of breath on my cheek that I loved so much.

Oh God, meningitis! I needed help. Annette. She'd make everything all right.

Holding Natasha tightly to me, I flew downstairs to the phone.

'Come round, Annette. Please. Now. Something's not right. It's Natasha. Please come. Oh God. She's too hot. Please help her.'

'I'll be right there.'

In my arms, Natasha made a gasping noise. Then the little unwanted girl who now meant everything in the world to me fell silent.

Karissa and Ricky were standing in the doorway, holding hands, looking at me. They could sense the badness in the house. 'Everything's all right,' I told them. 'It's all OK.'

I tried to make a deal with God. 'I know it's my fault. I know you are punishing me for being selfish. I understand that. But that was before I held my little girl. Now it's different. I love her. Don't take her away from me. She needs her mummy. She'll be lonely without me. If you give her back to me, I promise, promise, that I will look after her for ever. I will make her happy. Please give me a second chance. I need my beautiful girl.'

'Laura!' It was Annette. She was standing in front of me, two of her kids next to her. They were dressed up for a school play. Shepherds. As was usual, the front door had been unlocked.

'Give her to me, Laura. She needs a doctor. I'll take her. You stay here.'

I nodded. 'She's warm,' I said. 'She'll be fine.'

Annette gently took Natasha from my arms and ran out of the house. The doctor's surgery was only a few minutes away. I remembered about breakfast. In a daze, I fixed cereal for Karissa and a bottle for Ricky. I had to get hold of Dave to tell him what was happening. He was on site near his mother's house. I called her.

'Something terrible has happened.'

'Oh God, it's not Ricky, is it?'

'No, Natasha. She's . . . she's . . . Get hold of Dave, please. Tell him to come home.'

I then called Dawn and Mum at work and told them as best I could what was going on. 'She was unconscious. I think it's meningitis, but she's going to be all right. She was warm and making noises.'

Annette's kids took care of Karissa and Ricky in the kitchen. They were old enough to understand they had to help. They made sure breakfast was eaten and then tidied up and started a game. I stood at the lounge window looking for Annette and Natasha, full of self-recrimination.

If only I hadn't moved her out of our room just because I wanted some sleep. If only I had turned the heating down. If only I had gone in to see her first thing. She must have been frightened. She must have cried out for me. If only I had listened out for her. From now on, I will check on her before anything else. From now on, I will always know my precious girl is safe. She'll never be alone again.

Where is Annette? Why is she taking so long to bring Natasha back?

Dawn and Mum appeared at the same time. I said that the doctor would know what to do. I said that Annette had taken her straight there. I said that Natasha had been making noises. I said that she was warm. I said that she would be back home soon. What I didn't say was that the voice inside me was telling me something I didn't want to listen to. 'Natasha isn't coming home,' it whispered as I desperately tried to block it out. Then I saw Annette walking down the street. With a lady doctor. Without Natasha.

I had to speak before the doctor did. I had to stretch time for as long as I could. 'Don't say anything. Just tell me where my baby is and I'll go to her.' If I could have stopped the clocks, I would have.

The doctor reached out a hand to me. 'I'm sorry.'

I can barely say it now. I feel ashamed. But I have to confront it. The first thing that I felt when the doctor said those words was relief. I would be able to cope with my life again.

Then the moment overwhelmed me and I collapsed on a chair. I am told I was screaming Natasha's name, but I don't remember. The next few hours are a blur. Everyone seemed to be asking questions about what had happened, and when they weren't doing that they were crying. I know Dave and his mum and his sister came. I know everyone did their best to comfort me. I know I didn't think about Dave then, what he must have been feeling. All I was capable of thinking about was Natasha, and myself. My mind was in meltdown. I couldn't cope with Dave's grief as well.

The doctor left soon after she'd arrived. She had to get to the hospital. That was where they had taken Natasha. Not the Natasha whom I had loved and held, but the Natasha who had been carried out of this house, already dead.

After a while, my usual doctor arrived. He took me upstairs, away from the chaos and confusion, to explain as best he could. It had been a cot death, he said. They had done all they could to revive her, but it was too late. But what about the noises? She was alive when I picked her up. No, he explained, she had probably died at that moment. The noises were a reflex. She had already gone. He gave me some pills to try to calm me down, to help me sleep if possible. They didn't work and I was still awake and in shock when the police arrived.

I was walking down the stairs when they came into the

lounge. I'm not sure who opened the door to them. I saw their black shoes first, then their black trousers and then the uniform. It pushed me over the edge.

I couldn't understand what they were doing there. Why couldn't they leave us alone? They were encroaching on private grief and they had no right. The powerful cocktail of emotions inside me exploded and they received the full force of my anger. I shouted and screamed at them. In retrospect, I realise they were only doing their job, and in fact they were kind and polite and understanding. But I couldn't see that at the time.

They disappeared upstairs, reappearing a few minutes later. That was the moment when my heart snapped in two. It was years before it was mended again, and it was never the same. The police were taking away Natasha's mattress. She would never sleep on it again.

Chapter Nine
She Won't Be Coming Back

'Where's Baby? Can I play with Tasha?'

It was breakfast time and Karissa was asking the questions she had asked almost every morning since I'd first brought Natasha home from hospital. Karissa adored her little sister. She loved playing with her, stroking her, making her laugh. They were building a bond that I thought I would never see broken in my lifetime.

Karissa used to understand when I explained that Natasha was staying over at Lynne's. She was happy that Natasha was having fun with Auntie Lynne. This would be very different. I knew there was no point in pretending. It was our first real step in a life without Natasha. 'Baby has gone away, sweetheart. God called her. She's gone to heaven to live with him. She won't be coming back.'

Those last words were the hardest I had ever spoken. I couldn't hold back the tears and when Karissa saw me crying I could see she was about to start as well. She didn't understand what I was saying, but she could sense the upset. All I could do was hug her and try to reassure my beautiful daughter. 'Little Natasha is happy. She's where she wants to be. God will look after her. He'll play with her and make her smile. One day we'll see her again.'

I didn't really believe this. Ever since the church bells had made me sad, traditional religion had stopped playing a part in my life. I loved, and still love, the community feeling of a service, the sense of people coming together with a purpose to support one another. Today, I think I even believe there is a God, but not in the sense of a heaven where Natasha is. I think there must be a God that looks after us all; perhaps a guardian angel is a better way of putting it. I certainly believe someone must have been looking out for me all these years, otherwise I wouldn't be here. Back then, I just wanted Karissa not to worry about her sister.

'We can go to her room to say goodbye. She'll want to say goodbye to you too.' I took her by the hand and we went into Natasha's room. Her cot was a mess. The police had done their best not to leave the bedclothes lying around, but still, with the mattress gone, it looked all wrong.

'See?' I said to Karissa. 'Baby has taken her bed to God's house. Every time she goes to sleep on it, she'll think of us. Let's say goodbye together, shall we? Bye-bye, Baby. Sweet dreams.'

After that, Karissa continued to ask about her sister for a while, but in time she realised Natasha wasn't coming home. She missed her, but she was only three. Other things became important in her young life, which I was happy about.

With two children to look after, no matter what has happened you have to keep going. On Saturday, Dave and I took the kids to Asda. We needed food and it was time for them to have a look around and point out what they hoped Father Christmas would bring them. As we were walking through the aisles, a surge of guilt made my stomach lurch. A thought that I couldn't deny entered my head: this is much easier with two. It was the life I had wanted and I had it back. I hated myself and I didn't say a word to Dave, but I can't pretend I didn't think it.

A doctor whom both Dave and I knew, Dr Fleming, came to the house that afternoon. He was an expert in sudden infant deaths. He said that the post-mortem had been conducted and that the results confirmed cot death. He then did his best to explain what might have happened, but said that the medical authorities were only beginning to understand the contributory factors. He tried not to make us feel any more responsible than we already did, but it was difficult. Experts had identified various potential contributory factors that could lead to a cot death. We had virtually all of them.

The room was too hot. Dave and lots of our friends smoked in the house. Natasha slept on her front. She had moved into her own room before she was even five months old. This was all new to us. We couldn't have known; we thought we were doing the right things. But deep down, perhaps not so deep down, we felt guilty. I did, certainly. If I hadn't wanted sleep, Natasha would still be alive. What if it had something to do with me drinking down at the Legion when I was pregnant, even though I hadn't known?

As the realisation struck that everything I did wasn't always perfect, something dark took root inside me. I didn't notice it immediately, but it was there and before long it began to infect me. It took its time, first surfacing in the little ways I would react to things Dave said or did. Later, it began to engulf me, altering my mood and personality. I spent years recklessly trying to suppress it with alcohol and pills, until eventually I found hope and a purpose, which gave me the strength to confront the rotten growth and crush it. That was many years in the future.

Dr Fleming wasn't judging us; he was merely trying to help us understand and come to terms with what had happened. He recommended I continue taking the antidepressants I'd been given the day Natasha died, to help me through this incredibly difficult time. I did as he said, but they never really helped.

Dr Fleming told us that although Natasha's body had been released she would remain at the mortuary before being transferred to the funeral parlour. I was desperate to see her, to say goodbye, to kiss her one last time. I called the mortuary to ask when I could come in. They refused permission. They said it would be too distressing for me. I don't know whether they had been informed that I was on antidepressants and vulnerable or whether there was some other reason, perhaps because of the post-mortem surgery, but they said I would have to wait.

I saw her two days before the funeral. Before that, I endured an experience that no mother should ever have to go through. I had already bought some of Natasha's Christmas presents; they had been wrapped and placed underneath our tree, proclaiming my guilt every time I looked at them. I asked Dave to take Karissa and Ricky out for a couple of hours. I had to face this alone.

The reindeers and robins on the wrapping paper stared back at me sadly. I reached out and touched one parcel, then a second, then a third, imagining picking each one up on Christmas morning amid the squeals and laughter of a family and unwrapping them for Natasha as she sat next to me in her chair, uncomprehending but happy. Delicately, careful not to rip the paper, I unpicked the Sellotape and as each cotton dress, friendly teddy bear and woollen hat revealed itself, I held it to my face and wept. My little girl was never going to wear or play with any of them.

As I sat under that tree, one thought kept coming back to me, no matter how hard I tried to beat it away. Was the reason Natasha felt she had to leave me because she knew in my womb that she was unwanted? Throughout her short life, I had done my best to demonstrate that that was no longer true. Had I done enough?

Next, I had to deal with her beautiful little wardrobe, which sat lonely in her room. I could smell her on every item of clothing I removed. My heart broke all over again. When I could face it, I passed everything on to my brother Kevin, whose wife had recently given birth. He insisted on paying. 'Take it, Laura, please. Fifty pounds. It's worth a lot more. Buy Karissa and Ricky something special.' It was a generous gesture and I accepted. How could I deprive the kids of a treat? They had been through enough.

Dave and I had a heartbreaking decision to make. What

should Natasha wear on the day she was buried? We had agreed we were going to have her christened, even though we were not churchgoers. I'd been particularly keen. I wanted a family celebration, public confirmation of how happy I was to have my third and last child. A family occasion was still going to happen, but now it was for the worst possible reasons. Dave and I decided she should wear her christening gown, the same one I had worn and Mum before me. I couldn't bear the thought of taking it to the funeral parlour. Dave did it. I am sure it was no easier for him than it would have been for me, and I was grateful.

I went to see Natasha with my sister. Dave had tried to insist that he and I go together, but in the end I persuaded him to go with his mum. I said it was so he could support her, but really I thought it would be too distressing to be there with him. That dark seed of guilt had begun to push us apart, however slowly.

She would have been a beautiful baby at her christening. The dress was perfect. But she was no longer my Natasha. She had already gone; the still livid scar on her neck proved it. They had done everything they could to hide the brutal marks of the post-mortem, but it would have been impossible to do so entirely. I stood there looking at this tiny body, tears rolling down my cheeks, with Dawn clutching my hand in support, but I knew this wasn't my little girl. I gently kissed the top of her head, felt her hair brush my nose and understood this was the end. 'I promise you, sweetheart, I loved you the moment I saw you.' I murmured it under my breath and left.

There was one major issue that we had to sort out before the funeral. What to do about Dad? One evening when I was pregnant with Natasha, Dave and I had been sitting at home when, out of the blue, he'd turned to me and said, 'Why don't you give your father a call? Tell him you're pregnant. It's a good excuse. I know he hasn't exactly been Superdad, but I've been thinking about it recently. With Karissa growing up, I think it would be good if she knew her grandfather. And Ricky too. What do you think?'

It's strange how couples can sometimes have the same thought without either of them having said anything. I too had been thinking about Dad. And, for me as for Dave, it had been Karissa who had sparked off those thoughts. Whenever she did something exceptionally funny or cute, which was often, I would think how much Dad would have loved it. He had such a soft spot for girls; he would adore Karissa. 'You're right, Dave,' I said. 'I'm going to call his sister Margaret. She'll know where he is. It's about time.'

Dad was thrilled. We arranged to meet and, as predicted, he loved the kids, Karissa in particular. During my pregnancy, he saw quite a lot of them and he even offered to help out as I grew larger and larger, and became increasingly tired, by taking Karissa on the ferry with him to Ireland to meet his family. In a moment of madness, I agreed to the trip. I was pleased that he wanted to show his granddaughter off, but allowing my alcoholic father to take my daughter on a ferry across the Irish Sea? I put it down to my hormones and thanked God they made it back in one piece.

He was thrilled when Natasha was born and he came to visit us in the hospital. I made treble-sure that Mum, Dawn and the boys were not there at the same time. Therein lay the problem with the funeral. He was very much on the scene again, but what might happen if he attended? Shaun and Kevin were still full of resentment towards him, as was Mum. I understood that.

Mum bravely said it would be OK if I wanted him there. I thought about it. Emotions were likely to be running high. It would be the first time Shaun and Kevin would have seen him since we'd escaped to Sonia's. It didn't take a huge amount of imagination to picture what was likely to happen. I decided it would be better if he didn't come, and Dad was very hurt.

I should have told him myself, but, with so much going

on, I avoided the issue. I had a fair idea how he would react and I couldn't face it. Mum's brother Michael delivered the news that Dad wasn't welcome. When I spoke to him afterwards, he was bitter and resentful. 'Who the fuck is Michael to be telling me what I can do about my own granddaughter?' I understood his feelings and frustrations, but I was too weary to deal with them. I'm not sure he ever forgave me.

The funeral took place on a crisp winter morning at the local Patchway church. I have not been back to the grave since; I can't face it. It was a small, quiet affair, family only. I didn't take Karissa or Ricky. Afterwards, we went back to the house for sandwiches. Sonia helped, along with Mum and Dave's mum. People stayed for a couple of hours, and that was it.

The day was oddly mundane, but that didn't worry me. I had said my goodbyes previously. That chapter in my life was dealt with; it was time to move on. The hole Natasha had left would always be there, but Christmas was a week away and we had two children to make happy.

On Christmas Day, we decided to go to the Legion for a get-together before lunch. There would be a lot of people there, and Dave and I both thought it might do us some good and that the kids would have a lot of fun. Patchway is a small, tight community. Everyone knows everyone else's business and that made things easier. There was no having to explain to anyone that Natasha had died. We didn't need to pretend that everything was all right and everyone around us understood the situation. We ended up having a nice time. Karissa and Ricky loved seeing Father Christmas and there were crackers, hats, daft jokes and songs. It was a jolly atmosphere, except there was something, someone, missing.

A friend of ours had recently had a baby, back in September, and she had brought her along. She was sitting in a carry-seat by her mum. Every time I looked at the little thing, I saw Natasha. It was very hard, but I had to steel myself. That was the past. It might have been only a fortnight ago that Natasha had died, but it was still the past.

A health visitor called round to see me in early January, to check on how I was coping. I explained that I was fine, that the local community was being incredibly supportive. People offered to help with shopping, by taking the kids overnight, even cooking for us, and almost every day the doorbell would ring with a new delivery of flowers.

She warned me that this would not last and that I should prepare myself for when new local dramas overtook our tragedy and we were no longer the centre of attention. 'When that happens,' she said, 'it's very common to feel lost and abandoned. You should be prepared for that.' I understood what she was saying, but I knew it wasn't going to happen to me. How could it? I was too busy organising my wedding to have time to wallow in grief.

Dave had proposed to me the previous October and we had set the date for 25 April 1987. After Natasha's death, we discussed postponing the wedding but decided not to. What good would come of that, we reasoned. Natasha was going to have been a bridesmaid on the day, even though she would have been only nine months old. We would honour her by going ahead as planned. The last time we had brought the families together had been for Natasha's funeral; now we would give them something to celebrate. It was the right thing to do.

We didn't invite Dad for the same reasons he wasn't asked to come to the funeral. In fact, it would have been even worse at the wedding, as there were far more people invited, many of whom knew, or thought they knew, what Dad had been like. We were running a risk that a number of Mum's family would not attend, and that wouldn't have been right. They had provided a support network for Mum and for me. I would have liked Dad to have given me away, and he wanted to, but in the end it was not a difficult decision to make. The combination of Mum's family, my brothers, Dad and alcohol would have been too combustible. Dad once again took the news badly. I had sympathy for him, but I never wavered.

The wedding was a great success. We married in the Methodist church in Filton. Dave's divorce meant that the Catholic Church would not agree to perform the ceremony. I wore a beautiful cream dress. I was very proud and happy. I saw it as an important step towards the perfect life I had set out to make for myself. It was a family affair. Dawn was my maid of honour, Karissa was one of my bridesmaids, Ricky was a pageboy and two of my nieces were flower girls.

The floral display inside the church was stunning: wonderful bouquets on either side of the altar and sprays of spring blooms lining the aisle. Natasha was not forgotten amid the smiles and festivities. Before the reception, I asked Mum and Dawn to clear the church of the flowers and place them on her grave. I couldn't do it. Natasha's smiling face would have stolen the hearts of everyone at the wedding had she been there, but fate had not allowed that. Instead, her absence had broken mine. To have stood in that graveyard, next to her, in my wedding dress, would have been too much to bear.

Despite the sadness, it was a day on which I looked forward to a bright future. The party went on until the early hours and everyone enjoyed themselves. I was happy and content, for a month.

Prior to the wedding, I had made a second big decision – to have another baby. I had been fantasising about having another girl and when I closed my eyes I could see her, little Emma Lea. The name sprang from a song I loved to play at the time. It was an oldie I had discovered on a compilation album Dave had bought for me: 'Emma' by Hot Chocolate. It was a sad song about a young girl called Emmaline with dreams of becoming an actress. In the end, she couldn't take any more when she didn't make it. Perhaps I should have listened to the lyrics more closely.

I made an appointment to see my GP and by the time I walked into his surgery I was armed to the teeth with facts.

Reversing a sterilisation is not a simple procedure, but it is not impossible. I had done my research and I knew it could be done. I was also fully prepared to play the age card if necessary.

I explained to the doctor what I wanted and, while he was very sympathetic and understood the reasons for my decision, he gently explained that the success rate for such reversals was very low and that the procedure would not be available on the NHS. I had suspected this might be the response.

'That's ridiculous and unfair. I am 22, for God's sake. The NHS should never have performed the sterilisation in the first place. What was the hospital thinking? I was too young and vulnerable to make such a decision. I believed then that I couldn't cope with a third child, so of course I wanted to feel that I wouldn't have any more. But that wasn't what I really wanted. They must have known that. It's a basic human right to be able to have children and they took that away from me when I was too confused and distressed to fully understand the implications. I will fight with everything I have.'

The doctor agreed to put me on the NHS waiting list and to recommend that I have the reversal as quickly as possible. Still, it was going to be months, if not a year, before I would see the specialist to discuss the operation and, assuming that went OK, it would be at least another six months before the procedure itself would be undertaken. That was fine while I had the wedding to organise, but once that was over and the excitement had died down, I found myself anchorless and adrift, as the health visitor had warned. I understand now that I should have given myself a proper period in which to grieve, but I thought I was stronger than that, better. I wasn't.

There was nothing for me to latch on to, no excitement and no focus. I felt I was merely surviving, not living, an observer, not a participant. The kids would be playing or needing to be fed or washed, Dave would go off to work, or we would go to the Legion together, or I'd visit Mum and Dawn; the rituals of life were happening, but I wasn't engaging with them. They were going on around me, not with me.

I was unhappy and struggling not to let the darkness take over. I tried to increase the dosage of the antidepressants I had been prescribed. The doctor kept telling me I had to give it time, but I could feel myself slipping away from the people around me whom I loved. I had to do something to stop myself. I already knew the answer; I just hadn't been prepared to admit it until then: the painkillers I used to take. If I could get hold of some of them, everything would be fine.

It wasn't difficult. I was good at this. I told the doctor I was suffering terrible headaches. Migraines. I explained that they were so debilitating that I was unable to look after the kids when one came on. I was forced to lie in a dark room for hours, which meant Dave had to come home, which in turn meant he didn't earn as much money, which brought additional worries, resulting in more migraines. I needed help badly. It came in exactly the shape I wanted: blister packs of distalgesics.

I took two the moment I reached home after picking them up at the chemist. Almost immediately, I felt the darkness lift. I realised I was holding in my hands the answer to all my problems. An old friend had returned and was going to be around for a very long time.

Chapter Ten
We're in Trouble

My hand was trembling. It had taken many months to arrive at this moment. Consultations, discussions, more consultations, everyone telling me that the chances of success were minimal. But I knew better. I had decided what was going to happen. Now I just needed the line on the little stick to turn blue.

The hospital had called in the spring of the previous year, 1989 – two years after I'd first spoken to my GP about having the sterilisation reversed – to make an appointment for me to see a specialist. He tried to persuade me not to have the reversal, but I was adamant. I trotted out the human rights speech again, told him how my last chance at happiness had been stolen from me when I was vulnerable. I left him no choice. He agreed to perform the operation. I was put on a waiting list and after eight months I found myself once again drifting off under general anaesthetic in preparation for yet more abdominal surgery. It was not to be my last. I was told that the operation had been as successful as could be expected. My tubes had been reconnected, but the existing scar tissue could cause problems. All I could do now was hope.

The line turned blue. I'd known it would. I was going to have another baby. I was thrilled. This child was going to be the glue that would mend my family. Natasha had just come a year too early, that was why I hadn't realised how much I wanted three children. I'd been blind then to what the future should be, but now I knew for sure. Dave was pleased too, for me. He had counselled against the reversal, worried about how I would react to the likely disappointment, but he knew what I was like and recognised that I wouldn't be happy until I had what I wanted.

My GP confirmed what my home pregnancy test had told me. He did his calculations and I had a due date. In eight months' time, the hole that Natasha had left in my life was going to be at least partially filled. I wouldn't need any more pills after that. With both Karissa and Ricky at school, I would be able to manage far more easily than before. The timing couldn't have been better. I told my mum, Dawn, Annette, anyone who might be remotely interested in the wonderful news. I even told everyone at work. That was a mistake.

I was volunteering as an assistant at Karissa and Ricky's school. Ricky had found it hard going into reception class, and I had found home very lonely without him and Karissa. If they couldn't be with me, I had decided, I would be with them, and it was working well. I helped out in Karissa's class and was making friends with the teachers and other assistants. Within weeks, it was me who needed the work more than Ricky required me to be there.

A month after I had told everyone my news, I woke up early to discover the sheets of our bed soaked in blood. My blood. All the way to my GP's surgery, the bleeding continued, heavy. It could mean only one thing. I was having a miscarriage. My baby was gone. Fearing the worst, the doctor tested me, and when the results showed I was still pregnant, I felt a glimmer of hope. 'Bleeding like this can happen in the early stages,' the doctor told me. 'Especially after the surgery you've undergone, Laura. I won't pretend it isn't a worry, but all we can do now is monitor your condition very carefully.'

Four days later, I was still bleeding. There was nothing normal about this. I knew it and so did my GP. When I went back to see him, he referred me immediately to the hospital for tests.

'Laura,' the surgeon told me, 'I'm afraid it is as we suspected. You are not pregnant. Not properly. The scan shows it quite clearly. You can see here, if you want to. There's a rupture. That's what's causing the bleeding. We're going to have to operate straight away to remove it. We talked about this earlier, it's quite a simple . . .'

The surgeon kept speaking, but I stopped listening. Before they had taken me for my scan, he had sat me down and explained the various possibilities or, more accurately, the one possibility: an ectopic pregnancy, where the embryo is caught in the fallopian tube. Fairly common, apparently, when a sterilisation is reversed. I had been informed of that before I'd had the operation, seven months previously, but I was sure I would be the one to buck the trend and I had put it out of my head. Until now. My beautiful, family-saving baby wasn't real after all. Another fantasy.

They removed my tube altogether. They had to. Back home, I could feel myself beginning to slip away once more. I felt I was being toyed with, offered the chance of complete happiness only for it to be snatched away. The darkness inside me began to spread again, happy with the destructive force it was wielding. If I was to fight it, there was only one way: I still had at least a chance of having a baby to complete my perfect family.

In those first few days back home, my resolution wavered. I was physically and emotionally fragile. I wanted to stay positive, to believe that we could have another baby, but it was difficult. The world seemed to be closing in on me, squeezing the life out of me. I couldn't breathe and wherever I tried to escape, there was Natasha. No, that's not quite right. Natasha was gone; she wasn't haunting me. What I couldn't escape was the guilt of Natasha. The darkness was no longer confined inside me. It had taken over the house, calling to me in my darkest hours, reminding me that the house had killed my baby. When it almost claimed Karissa and Ricky as well, I knew we had to move.

Since Natasha's death, Dave had been working hard on home improvements. He knew it meant a lot to me. I think it was also his way of having something to focus on, to take his mind off the terrible tragedy for a short time at least. We had decided to change the whole configuration of the house. Previously, the toilet had been downstairs, with the bath and sink upstairs. Both rooms were small, so we decided to move the toilet upstairs with the sink, knock down the downstairs loo to give us more space and install a spa bath in the corner of our bedroom. Unconventional, but it made good use of the space available.

After my ectopic pregnancy, Dave could see I was struggling to come to terms with it and he did what he could to help cheer me up, which mainly entailed socialising with friends. Early one evening, three weeks after I had returned from hospital, I was getting ready for a night out. Dawn was coming round to babysit and I wanted to be dressed and have Karissa and Ricky bathed before she arrived. The kids were playing in the bedroom as I stole a quiet half-hour to myself, lying in the bath, trying to work up the enthusiasm to go out. The bubbles of the spa helped to relax me and I felt better as I stepped out of the bath, pulled a towel around myself and dried my hair in the mirror.

I refilled the bath as I stood there, ready for the kids to have a quick in-and-out while I got dressed. Finished with my hair, I scooped them up from their game and, in a flurry of giggles and laughs, they undressed and in they went amid the bubbles and toys. Bath time was never a problem with those two. They enjoyed splashing each other and playing monsters and having all sorts of imaginary fun that I could never follow.

I turned my back for less than a minute while I selected my clothes for the evening. I could hear their nonsense behind me. All was well. Laying out my skirt and top on the bed, I looked up expecting to see one of them covered in foam 'attacking' the other. Instead, I watched Karissa act out a scene that haunts me still.

She was kneeling in the bath. Ricky wasn't paying her any attention, finding his plastic submarine far too interesting.

She must have been getting bored. When I looked up, she already had it in her hand. The hairdryer. I had left it plugged in, lying on a seat by the bath. In the past, I had let Karissa help Mummy with her hair. She knew how to switch it on and off. In a second, the room was filled with the noise of a little girl's whoops of delight and the blowing of hot air.

The scream of horror reached my lips but went no further. If I frightened her, she might drop it into the bath. They were going to be taken away from me, as punishment for my carelessness, my selfishness, just as Natasha had been.

I tried not to panic. Moving round the bed with as calm a step as I could manage, I spoke in a measured voice: 'Karissa, sweetheart, that's Mummy's toy. Put it down gently on the chair like a good girl.' She was holding it in her wet hand, pretending to dry her hair. The shock might pass through her tiny body in an instant. 'Don't switch it off, because Mummy needs it now.' I didn't want her to touch the switch. 'Just put it down.'

Ricky was suddenly interested and made a grab for the hairdryer. He almost got his fingers on it, but I was ahead of him. I was near enough to move quickly, before Karissa could react with fright. I snatched it out of her hands. My babies were safe, but it was a warning. We had to leave that house.

I demanded that we move and within a month we were out. Working in the building trade, Dave knew a lot of people who could make things happen quickly. We found someone, a friend of a friend, to rent our house. The arrangement was a bit ad hoc. There was no direct debit or standing order for the payment of the rent. It was more like we'd get it when he had it. We should have been firmer about the financial side of things. It was a lesson we failed to learn over the next few years.

Dave also managed to secure a second mortgage for a house we had seen in Bradley Stoke. Back then, companies were falling over themselves to lend money. Everyone was being encouraged to be entrepreneurial, to take out loans, to improve themselves. Everything happened quickly and painlessly. We put in an offer, it was accepted, we moved out and someone moved into our old place, all within days. I felt liberated.

The school had been fantastically supportive after my operation, giving me time off and letting me know that I was welcome back as soon as I was ready. I had decided not to move the kids from their school. They were happy there. I figured they had faced enough disruption over the past couple of years. There was no reason to inflict more than was necessary. It was a ten-minute drive to school from the new house and, as I hadn't passed my test, the burden fell on Dave, but it wasn't a huge problem. The school was opposite Mum's house, and if he was ever running late to pick us up, I had a key to her place if she was out. It was easy for us to wait for him there.

Within days of starting back volunteering at the school, I was looking at a blue line again. But the elation I had previously felt did not accompany it this time. Somehow I knew I was not going to be given another child. I was resigned to the fact that I didn't deserve one. Heavy bleeding soon followed – while I was at school. I didn't need to be told what was happening. I called my doctor and agreed to go straight to the hospital after I'd explained to the school principal.

'Laura, please sit down,' she said when I knocked on her door. 'What can I do for you?'

'I'm ever so sorry, but I'm afraid I have to leave, right away. I have to go back to hospital.'

'Oh no, you poor thing. Of course. Go right away. It's none of my business, I know, but is it the same as before? You must feel awful. Let me call a taxi. We'll get you off straight away.'

That was what she said, but it wasn't what I heard. I felt guilty and I transferred it to her. In my mind, the moment I mentioned the hospital, she looked down her nose at me. 'Ah, I see. Pregnant again, are you? Been at it like a little rabbit? I suppose people like you can't help it.'

She wasn't viewing me harshly, but I felt she was. I panicked, lied. There was no way I was going to allow her to think I had been so reckless as to fall pregnant again almost immediately. 'It was twins. They missed my baby's twin the last time. How could they? And now he's gone as well. It's too awful to bear.' She didn't believe me. Why would she? It wasn't a feasible story. It put an end to my volunteering at school. I couldn't face going back again.

As a drowning woman clutches at whatever she can, I made a desperate attempt to persuade them not to remove my tube. I was convinced my baby could survive. But it was impossible. Inside a week, I was home again. My family circle would never be complete. The fault line was permanent and could crack open at any moment to expose my dark centre.

The summer drifted past in a blur. I found it impossible to engage with Dave, the kids, Mum, Dawn, anything. I couldn't see the point in making an effort when everything I touched seemed to wither away and die. I had no control over my own life. The only friends who understood me were my painkillers and the odd bottle of strong Diamond Blush cider. They didn't sneer at me or make unreasonable demands. They only wanted to help me feel better.

At least during the holidays Karissa and Ricky were at home and I was able to manage where they went and what they did. As soon as school restarted, I lost even that small amount of independence. I was once again reliant on Dave. Another granule of self-esteem was crushed. I had to find a way to assert myself. Dave provided me with the chance.

Work in the building trade had been steadily declining throughout the year. The recession was biting and Dave was beginning to feel it, although he was rarely idle. When not working, he would either be in the pub, down the Legion or renovating our house. We'd decided we wanted to put in a pond in the back garden before the winter set in. Dave was working hard on it one afternoon while Karissa and Ricky were at school in Patchway. It was 3.15 p.m.

'Dave, we've got to go. You know the kids will be waiting by the gates at 3.30. Come on.'

'Yeah, yeah.'

'Dave, put that down and get in the car. I don't want to be late.'

'All right, all right. Enough. I'm almost done.'

Fifteen minutes later, we were in the car and I was furious.

'Laura, for fuck's sake. They'll be fine. We're only going to be ten minutes late. The teachers will be there. There's no problem.'

What he was saying was true. The school did always look after the children of parents who were running late, but I didn't care. I tore into him. 'You don't get it, do you? Are you just thick or don't you care? I've had enough. That's it! You're a selfish bastard. I can't live like this any longer. The moment we get home, I'm leaving. For ever. I'm taking my kids and don't you dare try to stop me.'

I was as good as my word – the leaving bit, anyway, not the for ever bit. I called a taxi and Karissa, Ricky and I went off to stay with Mum. It made me feel empowered. I was doing something on my own. I was taking charge. Within a week, we were all back home, with me apologising and Dave promising never to be late again, assuring me that he understood the pressure I was under and that he would do everything he could to help. That satisfied me, for a short while. Then when Dave wasn't available to take me to the supermarket for the weekend shopping on a Saturday morning because he was working, that was enough. Back to Mum's for a few days before we once again made up. This went on throughout the whole of the autumn and into winter.

I wasn't being fair, but I didn't care. I needed to be in control and this was a way I could prove to myself that I was. It was unsustainable, because I didn't want to leave Dave, but for that short period of time it helped. Until bigger problems came along.

Over Christmas, we realised that our money worries were

more serious than we'd thought, and then it emerged that the person supposedly renting our other house, who had been struggling to pay, had left. Drastic action was needed and the only answer seemed to be for us go to live with my mum for a while.

I called Mum and she didn't hesitate. She'd had a spare room since Dawn had moved out. We could have that. It was going to be a tight squeeze, but it was the best we could hope for. I promised her it wouldn't be for long. Dave didn't relish the prospect of living under my mother's roof. He blamed her for all those times I had left him the previous year because she'd offered me a bolt-hole. He felt she should have said no when I'd asked to stay, that she should have forced me to sort things out at home instead of encouraging me. It caused a lot of tension, but we had to make it work.

We hired a van on Saturday morning, loaded up all our furniture, our television, everything we owned, and headed to Mum's. The kids thought it was a great adventure. Mum had a garage and we stored what we could there. We managed to sell the sofa and chairs to friends, which helped. At least we could give her some money for putting us up.

I was beginning to worry that we might be in even deeper trouble than I had thought. What if we couldn't clear our debts? Would we be sued? The more I thought about it, the more anxious I became. I needed something to help calm me down, something like the sleeping pills I used to pinch off Fang's grandmother. If only I could remember what they were called, I was certain I could persuade my doctor to give me a prescription.

I decided to find out. The old lady would be registered at the local surgery, so I rang up pretending to be her niece. 'If you could help, I would be very grateful. She's lost her tablets and can't remember what they're called. If we can't find them, I'll bring her round later to see about a repeat prescription, but if you could let me know what they're called in the meantime, that would be a great help. She's beginning to fret and it'll put her mind at rest if she knows what she's looking for.'

'Of course. Hang on a second. I'll check with the doctor.' There was a long pause before the receptionist spoke again. 'Can you please tell me again who is speaking? There seems to be some confusion.'

'What's the problem?'

'It's the name you gave for your aunt. She died five years ago.' I gave up on that idea.

Even with the money worries, I felt happy back at Mum's. It felt safe, an emotional and financial sanctuary for me. I was more in control there, even though it wasn't my house. I could walk the kids to school and Mum helped me look after them at the weekends. And she wasn't going to throw us out for not paying rent. Even Dave seemed happier, which was an unexpected surprise, given how he felt about Mum. Within a month or two, he started to talk positively about plans for a new line of work.

He reasoned that if no one was building new homes, then no one was moving. This meant there was more opportunity for loft conversions, extensions, that sort of thing. It made sense, and by summer, with the weather better, he'd started a new business that took off almost immediately. He was out a lot, which was probably the only reason Dave and Mum didn't kill each other, and the money began to flow in. He had his self-esteem back. He was buzzing and happy to go out with me to the pub, rather than disappearing on his own to drown his sorrows. I had my old Dave back again.

My general positive outlook was also helped by the fact that I was still taking my painkillers. They were my safety net if the animosity that sometimes reared up between Dave and Mum got too much. I kept my usage very quiet. I didn't take them every day, but I made sure I always had a supply. My own doctor was beginning to become suspicious of my merry-go-round of illnesses, the symptoms of which I had perfected, so I turned to a new source to supplement my supply – Dave's

GP. I called on his behalf, explaining I was his wife.

'It's rather delicate, I'm afraid,' I told the doctor when I was put through. 'Dave is too embarrassed to call himself. He finds it too awkward to talk about, but he's suffering a lot of stomach pain and it's forcing him to take time off work, which we can't afford. He needs some relief, well, in every sense. You see, he's constipated. He hasn't been for a week now. He's taking laxatives, but he's bent double with the pain. He tried some of my distalgesics and they appeared to help, but I think he'll need a supply of his own until it all comes out.'

I picked up 'Dave's' prescription within the hour, together with various suggestions for massage techniques to help move things along. This new supply gave me the breathing space I needed to throw my own doctor off the trail. It worked perfectly and I felt a degree of contentment I hadn't experienced in a long time. It wasn't real happiness, of course, but I wasn't willing to admit that.

We had been at Mum's for around five months when Dave came home and said he had met someone who would provide us with a mortgage based on his new income. It was above board and we jumped at it. By then, we'd got rid of the other two houses. Off we went house-hunting and we soon found a place, back in Bradley Stoke, that was on offer in a private sale. Three bedrooms, beautifully furnished, a garage, front and back gardens for the kids to play in: it was perfect.

The move was swift and painless. The house felt right. We had enough room, we didn't have to spend a fortune decorating or renovating, and I was determined not to make the mistakes of the past. This, at last, was going to be a proper home. Getting the kids to and from school had been a problem before, so I decided to move them to a church school near our new home. The timing worked well. In the new term, Karissa was moving up to the first year of juniors. I also learned to drive and when I passed my test Dave bought me a lovely little runaround.

To top it all off, I landed myself a brilliant job managing a kids' after-school and holiday club, which provided activities and outings while parents were working. The interview had been tough, in front of a panel of four, but I had decided I wanted the job and I made damn sure I got it. I had a week's notice and preparing for the interview became my latest focus. I had no need for pills as my ambition became all-consuming.

From the information supplied, I could guess the questions they were likely to ask. I read up on bullying, signs of abuse, first aid, techniques to capture children's attention. Nothing was going to stop me. If only I'd remembered in the years that were to come how liberating and exciting it felt to have such a strong sense of purpose, my life could have been very different. But I didn't remember and that self-awareness lay dormant for a long time. Back then, however, I was crackling with anticipation and energy. I was offered the job and I felt confident enough to stipulate that I was to be allowed to bring my own kids with me. They agreed.

With the kids settled at school, Dave's new venture going well and me enjoying freedom and a sense of self I had never experienced before, I at last felt I had cracked the code to the ideal life on which I had set my sights from the age of 16.

Then, less than a year later, Dave and I decided to go for a walk near Severn Beach and it was as though we kicked a pebble that started an avalanche of misery. At the time, we thought all our Christmases had come at once. We were the cleverest, luckiest people alive.

Chapter Eleven
Abandon Hope

It was a scene that could have been conjured up in Hollywood. The last rays of the setting sun were golden arrows ricocheting off a house made entirely of glass. That was what greeted Dave and me as we rounded a corner on the bank of the Severn Estuary at New Passage. We should have realised then and there that what we were seeing was make-believe, but we were star-struck. There was no going back.

I had been laughing at Dave's stories of fishing in this area when he was a lad. He was joking about the size of his catches. Arm in arm we walked; it was a perfect early summer's evening. Mum was looking after the kids, we had enjoyed a quiet drink and we were thinking of wandering back to the car – until the arrows shot back from the house and pierced us both straight through the heart.

On closer investigation, we discovered there were two houses on the site, each with windows on three sides, affording stunning views across the estuary. In the fading light, the water and the mudflats shimmered as though sprinkled with crystals. The span of the Severn Bridge was silhouetted against the red sky. There couldn't have been a more beautiful, peaceful place on the planet. We looked at each other and smiled. Someone must have fulfilled their lifetime's wish to be living here. Only no one was.

The two houses were clearly empty. No furniture, no signs of life. Was it possible they were for sale? Dave pulled at the sleeve of my jacket as I peered through the front window of the first house. 'Look, down there.' He pointed past the second house. 'There are two plots of land marked out. I could build on those.' He sounded like an excited schoolboy – worse, a giddy schoolgirl. 'I'm going to check them out.'

I pressed my face against the panes of glass, marvelling at the space and layout. The kitchen was visible, fully fitted but, I suspected, never used. Circling round the house, I came to the rear entrance, leading out to the garden. Stuck to the door was a notice. It should have read 'Abandon hope all ye who enter here'. Instead, it gave the name and telephone number of a property developer. I scribbled the details down and half an hour later we walked off, bewitched and powerless to stop the disaster rushing headlong to meet us.

Even though I knew that this was out of our league, that people like us didn't live in places like this, my heart was beating too fast for me to accept reason. I had to live there, no matter what. We talked about nothing else all night. I transferred all my hopes and aspirations for the future from the wonderful, happy home I lived in to a waterside mirage. We were only just pulling ourselves out of a financial hole, Dave was making good money and we were thriving as a family. At last, it was our time – and we were about to throw it all away. It was madness, but I couldn't stop myself. Neither of us could. We walked into the situation with our eyes wide open, like two naive children.

We called first thing the next day and discovered that the developer was actually a local solicitor. He agreed to see us and we met in his big, fancy executive office in the city centre, complete with mahogany-panelled walls, massive desk and leather swivel chair. We were impressed and he was straightforward in explaining the situation. He owned the houses and the plots, for which he had secured planning permission to build two six-bedroom bungalows. His intention had been to sell them once completed, but that was currently on hold because the builder he was using had gone bust. As for the houses, they were both mortgaged and were currently in negative equity – as a result of the slump in property prices, they were worth less than the loan he had taken out. He was holding on to them for the time being, until the market picked up. 'If you're interested in owning one of them,' he went on, 'this is the price I will accept.' He quoted a figure that instantly placed them beyond our grasp. The plots, however, were another matter.

Over a period of three or four months, a plan was developed that, on the surface, seemed to work for everyone. It was too easy. We were to rent out our home, with the tenant paying the mortgage direct to the bank. We would move into one of the completed glass houses, rent free. We all agreed it was better than leaving them empty. Dave was to build the two bungalows, paying for the labour and materials, and we would then secure a mortgage on one of them and pay the solicitor a sum we had agreed for the land, which would be considerably less than the value of the land plus bungalow. We ignored the one glaring problem: we had limited cash to undertake the building work. A detail, we told ourselves. We'll figure something out. We shook hands and the craziness was under way.

We were dizzy with excitement. At the kitchen table in Bradley Stoke, Dave and I would pore over the plans for the bungalow, refining and improving the layout and design. It was going to be the perfect family home and Dave was going to build it for us. There would be a massive master bedroom (en suite, of course), custom-designed rooms for the kids, a utility area, a living room with panoramic views – it went on and on, and every second was thrilling.

The more excited I became, the more I talked about it with family and friends. Everyone agreed it was a stunning location. Our enthusiasm was infectious and swept Mum and everyone else along with it.

As possible progressed to probable, Dave made a suggestion. If anything, Mum was even more enthusiastic about the location than us, and one evening, as we were once again discussing the minute detail of the layout, Dave said, 'Why don't we ask Maureen to move in with us? There's plenty of room, she loves the place, she would be a help for you with the kids and, with her job at the supermarket, she could help with the finances.' We put it to her and she was delighted. The plans were further amended to create a section towards the back of the house with a living room and an en suite bedroom, designed to provide her with some privacy and independence.

By November, everything was settled. It was time to turn words into deeds. We arranged our tenant, Mum gave up her council house and we all moved into one of the glass houses.

For the first couple of months, life was fantastic. My job was going well and whenever I stopped to think too long about how the hell we were going to be able to afford it, the ever-present pills took the edge off any rising worries. The darkness was being kept at bay.

Dave and I were still rowing, but that was how we were: two strong characters who weren't shy of making our feelings known, until, in the end, Dave always gave in and I got my own way. Over the years, I had perfected my tactics to deal with our arguments or punish Dave for any perceived wrong. I gave him the silent treatment and I was an expert. I would communicate about the kids if it was absolutely necessary, but other than that I wouldn't speak. I'd prepare our tea, but I wouldn't eat with him. At night, I wouldn't say a word in bed and I'd put the light out straight away. In the morning, over breakfast, nothing. I could keep it going for days. It must have been unbelievably frustrating, but I couldn't control my stubbornness and I didn't want to.

In the glass house, Mum acted as the peacemaker. If Dave was suffering the full blast of my silence, Mum would eventually intervene, quietly saying, 'Laura, he can't cope with you not speaking to him. There's so much going on, you need to work together, for the sake of the family.' That usually did it and we would be fine again for a few weeks. It might not have been the perfect marriage, but it was working, and we both felt we were moving forward on a great adventure.

Three or four months in, the first cracks began to appear. Cash flow. Dave had been able to afford the initial batches of material and to pay the labourers, but in the long term we couldn't continue to finance the building work ourselves, so Dave and the solicitor agreed a new plan. The solicitor would supply the funds for the building and pay Dave a wage. Once the bungalows were both complete, ownership of one would be transferred to us, following which we would secure a mortgage and pay him back everything we owed plus the cost of the land at the price originally agreed. What had seemed to us to be an irresistible opportunity to own an incredible building at a fantastic price was now carrying considerably more debt, but it still appeared to be a good deal. It was a worry, but we decided to press on.

By the following spring, our dream home had risen before our eyes: four walls, a roof, windows, plumbing. There was still a long way to go, and the second bungalow was further behind, but it looked as though we had made it. I named it Bridge View. A celebration was in order.

By that stage, we knew a number of people in the area. There was a wonderful village feel to the community; everyone knew everyone and we had been made to feel very welcome. I had never experienced anything like it before, the spirit and camaraderie, although in time it proved to be a curse rather than a blessing.

The local pub was the centre of the community and Dave and I enjoyed socialising there, Dave more regularly than me, both at lunchtimes and in the evenings. Together we had some great nights there and began to feel this really was home.

On his prompting, we agreed with the solicitor that we would move into our bungalow in April, and we planned a party for the weekend before. Lady Luck smiled on us. The sun shone all day during the preparations, and as the guests arrived the air was warm and the atmosphere happy. We hired a DJ, who set up his equipment on the sea wall overlooking the estuary. The sliding windows that looked out over the water were open all night and guests in fancy dress danced in the garden and living room as if it was one flowing space. We toasted our new home with champagne, our friends and family cheered, and Dave and I beamed at everyone, happy and proud of what we had achieved. We felt like millionaires. Within a fortnight, the facade began to crumble.

The first warning sign arrived when Dave drove past our house in Bradley Stoke and noticed all the windows were closed and the curtains drawn. In the warm, late-spring weather we were enjoying, that was odd. Having been burned in the past, this time we'd rented it to a relative and I insisted we go round the following day to ask what was going on. Ringing the bell and knocking on the door produced no result. Judging by the free newspapers and pizza delivery flyers we could make out in the hallway, no one had been home for some time.

Dave had brought his key with him and we decided to investigate. It no longer fitted the lock. If the alarm bells had been ringing before, they were suddenly accompanied by flashing sirens. Dave put his elbow through the glass pane in the front door and reached in to turn the handle. It was a struggle to push our way in, such was the pile of junk mail that had accumulated on the carpet. It didn't take long to figure out what had happened.

The place was empty: no furniture, no television, nothing. Our tenant had taken all his gear and disappeared. Worse than that, as we discovered when we sifted through the mail, he hadn't paid the mortgage from the day he'd moved in. The bank had written dozens of letters, all of which had been ignored. The most recent confirmed our worst fears. The bank had already instigated steps to repossess our house. Our bolt-hole if all else failed, our security, the one asset that was actually ours, the happy family home I had loved, was gone. We stared at each other in disbelief. This was just the beginning.

Before we'd moved into the bungalow, Dave had begun to notice that the supplies of materials he requested from the solicitor were taking longer to arrive and the deliveries were not always complete. He hadn't thought much of it initially, but when his routine request for authorisation to pay electrical subcontractors was turned down, we began to worry.

Finances were tight. The payment of Dave's wage became erratic and soon ground to a halt. We found ourselves in a desperate situation. The lack of funds meant Dave couldn't pay contractors, resulting in further delays, which in turn increased our debt as penalties were imposed by the solicitor, who was keen for at least one bungalow to be in a saleable condition as soon as possible.

Overnight, we were back in the financial abyss. With the bungalow incomplete, we couldn't obtain a mortgage; without a mortgage, we couldn't pay off our mounting debts. Mum and I were both earning, but not to the extent that it would help us out of the fix. I felt trapped by the weight of the financial problems. I couldn't see a way out and retreated into my shell.

I pushed everyone away except my old friend who never let me down: my painkillers. For a few hours during the day, they allowed me to pretend that everything was going to be fine, that Dave would work it all out. Soon, I was introduced to a new friend who would help me through the night: alcohol. Up to then, my drinking had been social. Very rarely would I drink at home. All that changed as the pressure began to build.

Dave's escape was the pub. As our rows intensified and home life became increasingly unpleasant, he sought refuge with the friends he had made locally. I began to suspect that there was more to it than that. It wasn't only the convivial atmosphere that attracted him. I felt sure he was having an affair.

The pills and alcohol helped blank out my suspicions. I felt I needed the support they gave me more than ever. I still had my catalogue of ailments to present to the doctor – backaches, period pains, migraines – and I kept these in a fairly constant rotation in order to ensure my supply. As had happened previously, the doctor was worried about the regularity of my prescription requests, but, as I had changed surgeries when we moved, he wasn't aware of the extent of my history. My records should have been transferred, but the system was slow and inefficient and I knew it would be months before they caught up with me. In the meantime, I made the most of it, sometimes claiming either that I had lost the original prescription or that the tablets had been stolen or mislaid.

The dosage was eight tablets, two taken four times daily, but that didn't give me the hit I craved. Instead, I began taking all eight at once, on an empty stomach for maximum impact and a longer high. My normal routine during term time, when I was working in the afternoons only, was to take them half an hour before lunch. I convinced myself that this was the only way I could be on top form. During the school holidays, when I was at the club all day, I used to sneak off to the toilets mid-morning and knock them back in one of the cubicles. No one knew a thing about it.

The buzz the painkillers gave me lasted until early evening. The second stage of my routine then kicked in, and it became a ritual I couldn't live without. At 7 p.m. sharp, I would be at our local convenience store, which had a small off-licence section, to buy the cans of strong, cheap lager that would see me through the night. Back home, I would slump on the sofa with the vaguely watched television for company, drinking the cans as quickly as I could. By 9 p.m., the financial worries would have disappeared and the pain of my crumbling marriage would have receded. Half an hour later, I would be dead to the world, slumped unconscious across the sofa. Mum would just about manage to shake me awake long enough for me to stumble upstairs to bed. I was lucky if I undressed. I never washed my face or brushed my teeth. That was beyond me.

Mum grew extremely concerned about my behaviour, but there was nothing she could do. If she gently tried to raise the issue of my drinking, she found herself on the receiving end of a stream of abuse: she was living in my house; she should stay the fuck out of my life; it was none of her business. Quickly, she learned to keep quiet.

Hiding from the mounting debt didn't make it go away. In the rare moments when Dave and I were not at each other's throats, we talked about it. We knew we had to do something to bring in extra cash. Our present might not have been very happy, but we still had hopes for the future.

Dave came up with the idea of running a basic B&B from the second bungalow. Work had begun the previous year, 1992, on the Second Severn Crossing and the construction companies were desperate for accommodation. He put the idea to the solicitor, explaining that we would pass on the money we made, which would chip away at our debt. It was a good idea and would buy us some time, but the burden of changing the sheets and making breakfasts fell on me. I began to feel overwhelmed, making the need for pills and booze even greater. I was trapped, with no means of escape from myself, and things were about to become even worse.

The letter arrived at the end of September. The mother of a lad who came to the after-school club had lodged a complaint about Ricky bullying her son. I was instructed to attend a meeting of the committee that presided over the club in order to explain what had happened. It seemed to me that this was taking things too far. Ricky and the boy had been in a couple of fights. They didn't get along with each other, that was all. The staff knew all about it and had tackled it appropriately. I felt that there was no reason for the committee to deal with the matter with an official meeting. I suspected their response had nothing to do with Ricky and was all about me. I got a feeling that the committee were aware of my drinking.

However, I couldn't believe I'd let it show. They had no idea about how I spent my evenings and my alcohol consumption never once spilled over into my work. I loved my job – it was the one thing in my life that gave me a sense of identity – and I was very conscious of always being sharp and alert when I was there. The pills helped with that, and no one knew about them either. If anyone had informed the committee, it would have to have been someone who had either seen me buying my cans or someone who knew me. I couldn't prove it, but I became suspicious and so the meeting seemed like a farce to me. It felt from the outset as if it was a witch-hunt. Rightly or wrongly, I felt ignored, as if they were going through the motions, not listening to any explanations, just waiting for one more incident they could use to get rid of me. 'Kids are here to be looked after, not hit,' I was told. 'If it happens one more time, we're going to have to let you go.'

I couldn't watch Ricky the whole time he was at the club, and I couldn't exclude him from being there. He was too young to be left at home on his own. I spoke to him about his behaviour, but he said he was only standing up for himself when he was teased about being small. I asked him not to react and he said he would try hard. But kids are kids. They constantly needled each other and it was always going to spill over again.

Within a week, another fight broke out and the noose tightened around my neck. Two days later, there was more pushing, shoving and tears, and within twenty-four hours I received a second letter, terminating my employment with immediate effect. Even though I had known it was coming, seeing it there in black and white was shattering. A lifeline had been snatched away from me, leaving me with nothing but a sense of worthlessness that grew more deep-rooted throughout the winter.

During those dark, cold months, Dave and I did little more than exist, following the patterns we had established over the summer. Pills would see me through the days and alcohol brought the welcome nothingness of collapse every night. The kids didn't understand what was going on, but, in the way children do, they learned to deal with it. However wretched I felt in the mornings, I was always up to make breakfast and take them to school. I convinced myself I was functioning as a parent.

We continued to provide accommodation for the workers on the Crossing, but by Christmas I had given up the breakfasts. Basic cooking facilities were available, which allowed the men to make themselves tea and toast in the morning, and I laundered the sheets and cleaned at weekends. All they cared about was having a bed to sleep in. The proximity to their work was more important than egg and bacon, and everyone seemed satisfied with the arrangements.

During the day, Dave did what he could with the bungalows, but it was slow going. Weeks would go by with no progress made, partly as a result of the weather but mainly because the required fixtures and fittings failed to materialise when they were due. But we were at least limping towards the salvation of a mortgage.

When he wasn't working, either on the bungalows or increasingly on other sites locally, Dave would be in the local. By now, I was convinced he was having an affair, but whenever I confronted him, he denied it. Fierce arguments would follow, but these fights achieved nothing other than to upset me and the kids. I had to avoid that if I could, so I allowed my addictions to dull the pain and anxiety.

The sense of injustice I felt at losing my job kept forcing itself to the surface. I was being punished because Ricky and another boy didn't like each other. That was crap. It was an excuse, not a reason. Someone had wanted to cause trouble for me and they had succeeded. My pride wouldn't allow that. I had been good at my job and had put a lot into it, trying to make the club better, the activities for the children more fun, the hours and accessibility easier for the parents.

Ashamed

I'd known what was required to make it a success, but my hard work had come to nothing.

The more I thought about it, the more it became a sore that wouldn't heal. I became obsessed with the idea that I couldn't sit back and let them get away with it. I was convinced I was better than the people who had sacked me. I began to make plans to set up a rival scheme. I didn't care how long it took; I was going to show them. Once again, I had a purpose in life and it made me stronger. The blister packs of pills and cans of lager took a step, a small step, backwards.

In June 1994, Dawn suggested we take advantage of the half-term holiday and go off for a few days with the kids to North Wales. Dawn had two children by then. Mum had already agreed to go to a caravan site with Sonia and Andy, and Dawn's plan was that we would join them. I liked the idea – a break from the pressures at home was just what I needed – but I wasn't sure it was going to be feasible. Dave had always been very resistant to the idea of me staying away overnight with the kids.

His reaction when I broached the subject took me by surprise: 'That's a good idea, Lor. You should go. Hopefully I'm going to be flat out here anyway. If I can get stuck in now, we might be able to finish off here within weeks. Have fun. You deserve it. The sooner we can sort out the mortgage, the quicker we'll be free.' It made sense, and although I was suspicious of his motives, I told myself perhaps I was being unfair. Maybe this time I really was being paranoid, imagining things that weren't there.

The holiday was a great success. Away from home and with my new business plan taking shape, I felt relaxed. Playing with the kids, going for long walks, visiting local attractions and having hectic family pub lunches all kept me active and focused. I found I didn't need my pills to the same extent while I was there. I would take a couple mid-morning to take any edge off, but that did me. There was no time to think about all the dark aspects of my life. I wasn't able to shake the need for my cans at night, however, but, as we were all together, chatting and having laughs, it was less obvious that I had a problem. I would still pass out before anyone else, but that was put down to holiday excess. Mum knew differently, but she didn't say anything. I think she was just pleased to see me smile for a change.

The only ripples in an otherwise peaceful and enjoyable week came when I tried to contact Dave. The caravan site had payphones near the shop and laundry area, and I would try to call home before we cooked the kids' tea, in the late afternoon, when I knew he'd have finished working. Whenever we spoke, Dave sounded vague about what he had been doing and where he had been. When I asked specific questions, he became evasive and whenever I said that I would try to call later, he wanted to know exactly when. As if, I thought, he needed to make sure that he was home or that someone else wasn't. The worries I had dismissed earlier began to gnaw away at me again.

Dave was cooking a welcome-home meal when we arrived back. Seeing him in the kitchen was unusual enough, but cooking? Something was wrong. I unpacked our bags downstairs, put a wash on and went up to our room. The duvet was pulled over the bed, but it wasn't right; it was at an angle, too far over on one side. I pulled it back to rearrange it and saw the mess of the sheet below. It was rucked up and loose at the corners. It looked as though someone had been fighting on it. One of the pillows had fallen off the far side. This was not the bed of a man who had been quietly sleeping on his own all week. Or at least that was my suspicion. I could tell we were drifting apart. I was not pleased with the way I was behaving. I was pushing him to be unfaithful, if he wasn't already, and I was looking for any signs of infidelity.

'Bit rushed this morning, were you? No time to make the bed, was there? Or were you too tired after all that physical exertion first thing? What little slut have you been entertaining?' Once again, he denied everything. He *had* been in a rush, that was all. How dare I accuse him? He was working hard to make a better life for us all. He was hurt and upset that I should say such things.

It was a convincing performance and for a moment I almost believed it – for a moment. It made me feel sick. The restorative effects of the holiday were gone in an instant. For a week, I had convinced myself I was part of a tight family. What was the point? I was living a lie and I knew it.

I didn't let up at all over the following days. Any chance I got, I would snipe at Dave. I tried to stop him leaving the house at night. In my drunken state, I would stand, or sway, by the front door, blocking his exit. We would shout and swear at each other and eventually he would call me a worthless, drunken bitch and barge past. Slumping down the wall in tears, I would crawl back to my cans.

The atmosphere in the house was toxic. No relationship could survive it.

Chapter Twelve
Please Come Home

'You killed her. You killed my baby. Natasha would be here today if it wasn't for you. I hate you for taking her away from me.'

Even as I said the words, I knew I had gone too far. I'd been drinking all day and was in a foul rage. It was only a few weeks after I'd returned from holiday to discover the unmade bed. I had got it into my head that Dave had been deliberately dragging his heels finishing the bungalow to ensure that money was tight and I was forced to stay locked up at home, leaving him free to go off and see his girlfriend. It didn't make sense, but I wanted to blame him for everything that had gone wrong in my life, and from there my anger escalated out of control.

I had drunk more than normal the previous night and had no recollection of going to bed, but when I woke that morning I was in my underwear, so perhaps Mum had helped me. Dave had slept downstairs. I couldn't blame him. I had wet the bed. I had no recollection of needing a pee, but my knickers were soaked, as were the sheets. The room stank and I was humiliated. I fought back the only way I knew how: I drank even more and lashed out.

It was all Dave's fault, I thought. He'd driven me to this state. The moment he walked in the door, I unleashed all my pent-up frustrations at the wreck my life had become. I called him a useless father, a waste of space who couldn't provide for his kids, only half a man who had to use whores for sex

– whatever I could think of that was evil, mean and hurtful. I didn't care that it wasn't true. He retaliated, taunting me with the fact that I'd wet myself.

We'd had rows before, but this time a line was crossed. Neither of us held back. I threw at him whatever I could lay my hands on; he grabbed me angrily by the arms in an attempt to stop the barrage of missiles. We were face to face, inches apart. That's when I said he'd killed Natasha.

He let go of me. 'That's it. No more. I'm leaving.'

That was all he said. He went upstairs, threw some things in a bag and was gone. I was too proud, or stupid, to say I didn't mean it. Instead, I pretended not to care. I slammed the door behind him in a sad gesture of defiance. I was glad Mum was out. I didn't want anyone witnessing the confirmation that I had ruined everything. I sat back down on the sofa, finished my can and opened another one.

Dave went to stay with friends. For the following week, he and I barely communicated. Karissa and Ricky seemed to take it in their stride. They had seen a lot in their young lives. I persuaded myself that this was just another incident they would deal with. My attitude had always been 'if I am all right, they are all right'. My pills were excellent at masking the truth. In reality, I had broken the promise I'd made to Karissa when she was born: I had not shielded her or her brother from alcohol, rows and misery. Instead, I had introduced those unwanted guests into our home, and during the years to follow they became persistent and damaging visitors.

I had no contact with Dave over this period and no desire to know anything about how he was living or what his plans were. Not until a letter arrived for him from a travel agent. Where the hell could he be going? I didn't hesitate to open it.

Bloody Majorca. It was a confirmation notice; he was to pick up his ticket at Gatwick that morning. I knew the couple he was staying with were going away for a week. It all fell into place. Dave was going with them. I could hear the conversation.

'Dave, you've been through the mill recently. You need a break. Why don't you join us? There's plenty of room in the apartment.' What a load of bollocks. I wasn't going to let that happen.

I rang the airport. 'I urgently need to put an announcement out over the tannoy.' I gave them Dave's name. 'Please say his wife needs to speak to him at home immediately. There has been a family emergency.' I waited for half an hour. Nothing. He was ignoring me. I wasn't finished yet. I called back, making up wild stories about Dave being wanted by the police and claiming he was trying to flee the country – anything I could think of that might cause him to be detained and miss his flight. My task completed, I sat down and had another drink.

I learned on the Sunday that he had not gone. I bumped into our new neighbours and they mentioned that they had seen Dave in the pub at lunchtime. I was delighted at how clever I had been. So delighted, in fact, that I decided to celebrate by starting drinking early. My buoyant mood did not last long. Memories of the day Dave had first moved in with me and his daughter, our daughter, Karissa, wouldn't go away. It was meant to have been the beginning of a fairytale. Was that now lost for ever?

I woke at three in the morning. I had to see Dave. If there was a chance of resurrecting our marriage, I had to try. For too long, I had been pretending not to care what was happening, drinking myself into denial. The truth was I had been at my wits' end for months. Now I felt oddly alert – no hangover, no fuzzy brain. I could see the way forward clearly.

I drove the few minutes to the house where Dave was staying. If the kids heard me leave and woke up, it wouldn't be a problem; Mum was home. I banged on the door until Dave sleepily opened it. Behind him, I could see his sheets and pillow on the sofa.

'Dave, we have to talk. I don't know what's going on any more. I can't go on living like this. I don't understand how this has happened to us. Please come home.'

'I can't. The person I married isn't there any more. The drink and pills have taken her away. I can't cope with who you've become, the anger and the poison. You have no self-respect left. I don't know how to stop you ruining your life, but I won't let you ruin mine or the kids'. If I come back, you might be OK for a week, but I know you. You'll start again and we'll begin fighting. It's destroying Karissa and Ricky. You have to sort yourself out.'

I wasn't going to beg. I nodded, got back in my car, drove home and went to bed. When I woke the next morning, there was only one thought in my mind: we had passed the point of no return.

I rang up the solicitor to tell him what was happening, that Dave had moved out.

'Is it for good?' he asked.

'Yes, we're finished. It's over.'

'Well, then, Laura, things are going to have to change. You must see that. You're not paying any rent and if Dave has gone I can't see how you'll ever get a mortgage. You're going to have to move out and I'm willing to help. I'll look for somewhere for you to stay.'

I knew the dream was over then. I was pinned in a corner with no escape and no one to turn to. I felt as though I was dying inside. 'That might be for the best,' I said.

We were caught in a vicious circle and I began to realise that the future I had envisaged was never going to happen. I wasn't about to move until I was ready and happy with what was on offer.

'I've got good news and bad news.' It was the solicitor on the phone. 'I'm going to take over the running of the B&B.' I wondered if that was the good news. 'So there will be no more money coming to you from there.' He was implying that somehow we had been fiddling the books, but I ignored the jibe. I was too worn down to defend myself. If he wanted to take cheap shots, let him. I had much bigger things to worry about.

'On a positive note, I have found a place for you to live with your mum and the children, a bungalow in Downend. I know the owners and they're happy for you to rent it.' Maybe this would be it, I thought. Yet another fresh start. I didn't want to leave my lovely house, but life was becoming intolerable. If the new place was clean and liveable, I would go for it.

Mum and I went to look at the bungalow, but it was damp and musty. I was under pressure to say yes, but it wouldn't have been fair on the kids. Apart from the condition of the property, they were going to have to share a room, which wasn't ideal with Karissa approaching eleven and Ricky nine. I decided to stay where we were for the time being.

As summer shifted to autumn, I couldn't stop myself wondering if there was a glimmer of hope that things between Dave and me might just turn around. But even if there was a chance, did I really want to grasp it? The question was complicated by the fact that I was now back in contact with Alan.

A friend had called three weeks previously to say she had bumped into Alan in a pub and he had asked for my number. He had heard rumours about Dave and me. She'd told him she had to speak to me first.

'Next time you see him,' I said, 'don't give him my number but get his.'

A couple of weeks later, she did, and after I had taken Ricky to his karate class one evening I rang Alan and we met outside some shops. We sat in his car chatting until it was time to pick up Ricky. It was good to see him. He was kind and calm and understanding. Talking with him stripped away many difficult years and reminded me of the hopes and dreams I used to have when I was younger. When he asked, I agreed to go out for a drink with him, and I told Mum all about it when I was pissed later that evening. I thought she would be pleased for me.

By the beginning of November, I had seen Alan three or

four times. Nothing had happened between us, but I was enjoying myself. He made me laugh. Our get-togethers were moments of relief from the difficulties at home. I was still taking my pills on a daily basis, still coming up with a variety of excuses for the doctor, but at least when Alan and I went out I didn't drink. I looked forward to meeting up with him and he seemed to like being with me. That alone gave me a sense of self-worth.

One day in the middle of the month, Dave came round so that we could talk about the kids. At first we were getting on fine, but before long we began to argue. Mum wasn't working until the afternoon shift and as Dave and I began to raise our voices, she came into the room. 'Look at the two of you. You can't spend two minutes together without having an argument. The whole thing is madness. Think what you're doing to yourselves. You're splitting up and your poor kids are in a mess.' She turned to me. 'As for you, you're drinking yourself into an early grave. And you' – it was now Dave's turn – 'you're off living a single man's life. What about the kids? You're throwing everything away. And now your wife is going out with her ex, Alan.'

I couldn't believe she'd said it. Dave hated Alan, and Mum knew that.

'Is that right? Well, you tell him from me that I'm going to go down there and kill him for messing with my wife.'

Dave stormed off and I kept thinking, 'Why did you do that, Mum?' I guess it was an attempt to bring us back together, but it was misguided. Dave was in a rage and I had to warn Alan. 'Let him come,' he said when I called to let him know what had happened. Dave didn't go round there, thank God. The last thing any of us needed was a fight. Who knows what might have happened? It could have been very ugly.

A few days later, Dave called the house. 'We have to speak, Laura. Let's go for a drink. For Karissa and Ricky's sake.' I agreed. I didn't take much persuading. Even after everything that had happened, I still loved him.

We met in a pub neither of us had been to before. It was neutral territory, which would make it easier. I decided not to drink. If we were going to discuss the children, I needed to be level-headed. It also gave me the opportunity to rub his nose in it and keep him on his toes. At the bar, when he asked me what I wanted, I replied, 'Just a Coke.'

'You don't want a lager?'

'No, just a Coke. I hardly drink when I'm out these days. Alan doesn't like it.' Ouch.

I knew Dave hated it when I was smashed and acting up, but he surprised me that evening when he also brought up my pill-taking. I'd thought, naively, that I'd kept it secret. I had been deluding myself, on many levels.

'You're going to kill yourself, Laura. You're popping pills constantly, on top of the drink. If there was a fire, none of you would get out because you would be too far gone. I'm worried about you, and Karissa and Ricky. I know things have been difficult between us, but all I've tried to do is provide for you and the kids.' He was very tearful. Then came the bolt from the blue. 'I've been thinking about this for a long time now. Lor, I don't want us to break up.'

That did it. We both opened up like we hadn't done in years. We talked for hours, about the kids, about the mistakes we had made and about ways of getting out of the hole we were in. He again denied having an affair. I wanted to believe him. I should have realised at that moment that this was not a reconciliation based on solid foundations.

He said he wanted a family Christmas and asked if he could move back in. I agreed. 'You won't regret it,' he told me. 'We'll have the best time.'

The first couple of weeks back together were great. In the run-up to Christmas, we decorated the house and bought a tree. The kids were happy their dad was home and we both made an effort. What Dave had said about my not being in a fit state to do anything if there was a fire had made an impact on me. I managed to cut down on the pills, but I found the booze harder, and I wasn't helped by the fact that as an early Christmas present Dave bought me a crate of lager.

Oddly, the one thing that did help with my alcohol intake was that Dave and I were socialising again. I found sipping my drink in the pub a lot easier than slowing down at home. I was wary of making a scene in public, which meant that I was more alert when we were out and, unfortunately, I sometimes heard things I'd rather have missed.

In the week before Christmas, I was standing chatting in the pub with a group of regulars while Dave was off entertaining another crowd at a table. One of the blokes, a bit the worse for wear, leaned over and said in an unsubtle drunken whisper, 'You do know Dave is shagging her, don't you?' He tilted his head towards Tracy, a young girl in her late teens whom I barely knew.

She overheard and put on a shocked, defensive expression. 'What's he on about? He's always talking crap. Miserable git. He can't handle his drink. Ignore him.' She wasn't a very good actress. My thoughts turned to that crumpled bed. I didn't want to believe it.

I felt as though I had been punched in the stomach. Once again, my attempts to create a picture-postcard life, complete with a special Christmas with carols, decorations and presents, had been built on a lie. I didn't know what to do. I couldn't face the trauma of confronting him. Instead, I turned to my pills.

After weeks of cutting down, the buzz they gave me was horribly, addictively glorious. They transported me to a fantasy land where my after-school club would soon take off and give me financial freedom, where Dave and I lived happily ever after.

Chapter Thirteen
I'm Nothing Without Them

Over the New Year period, I did my best to keep the family together, to try to create a bond between the four of us that Dave would never want to break. I failed. Dave wanted to escape and my drinking provided him with the opportunity.

What happened after I collapsed at around nine o'clock each night was an unknown world. Sometimes during the day I'd answer the phone only for the person on the other end to hang up, or in the night, half awake, I'd hear the sound of gravel crunching as a car crept up the driveway – clues that I steadfastly refused to consider. I was like a child with my eyes tight shut and my fingers stuck in my ears, blocking out the world.

We didn't go out to celebrate on New Year's Eve. I said to Dave that I wanted us to stay in, as a family, to bring us luck for the coming year. I tried hard to stay awake until midnight but blew it. By ten o'clock, I was gone. On New Year's Day, I had a vague memory of Dave helping me upstairs to bed. I didn't know whether he'd spent the rest of the evening at home or not and I didn't ask. I was too disgusted with myself. I wanted to make amends, to try to keep us all together, and I suggested that he and I go out for a quiet drink together that night.

We got on well, like old times. Although I restricted myself to only one drink, the evening flew past and we stayed until closing time. When we arrived home, Dave said he was going to stay up. 'But you go on, Lor,' he said. 'It's late.'

'Let's go to bed together for a change,' I said. That surprised him. 'We can watch television for a while if you want. I'm not tired.' I was used to my lager knocking me out cold. Having been very careful all evening, I felt wide awake.

'Why would you want to do that? You're never up this late. It's better if you go off now. I'd rather watch the TV on my own.'

That hurt. He was acting very strangely. 'But I'm not sleepy. I feel fine.'

'Well, then why don't you have a drink?'

Now I was really suspicious. Normally, Dave never suggested I drink at home. This on top of the crate of lager he'd given me before Christmas told me something was going on.

'There's some cans in the fridge you can have. I think I'll go for a little drive. I fancy looking at the stars.'

That sounded like a load of crap. 'That would be lovely. I'll come with you. Where do you want to go?' There was no way I was letting him out of my sight.

He was irritated. 'For fuck's sake, let's not bother. It's too late now anyway.'

'No, come on.' I took the keys and headed for the door. He had to follow.

'I'll drive,' he insisted.

As we drove up the lane to the main road, he tried to distract me, but it didn't work. There she was, waiting for him. Tracy. He drove straight past as if he hadn't seen her.

The next day, Monday, 2 January, the doctor's surgery was still closed for the holidays. I had none of my pills left and was reduced to trying a cocktail of whatever medication we had in the bathroom cabinet, which only left me feeling sick. I had arranged a couple of days previously to take Karissa and Ricky, together with our neighbours' two kids, to McDonald's for lunch. It was the last thing I felt like doing, but I had promised. Their mum and dad had arranged to go out for the afternoon and I was looking after them. Dave was supposed to be meeting his mates for a pint. I was taking an age to get ready and Dave was trying to hurry me up, looking increasingly jittery.

Fifteen minutes late, I had my act together. Dave had waited for me and as I reversed out of the drive I flashed him to go ahead in his car. He waved me on. When I got to the top of the lane, there she was again. Without my pills, the darkness inside threatened to engulf me. I felt as though there had been a death in the family.

I was in a daze at McDonald's. I knew the end had finally come. Dave must have called her from the pub the previous evening, while we were meant to be having some time to ourselves, just the two of us. That was a joke. The three of us, more like.

I couldn't pretend any longer. I had to finish the lie I was living once and for all. Somehow I got through the afternoon. Dave was already back when I returned home. I didn't speak to him. Mum made Karissa and Ricky something to eat and I started drinking.

At about eight o'clock, Dave said he was going out for a quick drink and would be back soon. I won't go into detail about it here, but that evening I followed Dave and caught him with his new girlfriend.

My heart was broken and I was angry. I wanted to get home as quickly as possible and for him to stay away from me for ever. Suspicion and the naked truth are worlds apart. I felt ashamed, foolish, small and weak. I had no home, no husband, no life.

The next day, I told Mum what had happened. 'It's just the four of us now, Mum,' I said.

'I wish I was surprised, Laura. But at least we know now where we stand.'

She was right. I told myself I would never pretend ever again. Another promise I didn't keep.

The next few days were horrible. Dave moved out and found a place nearby with Tracy. It seemed every time I was out in my car I saw her. It made me feel sick, as though she had beaten me. I wanted to get as far away from them as I could, but it wasn't practical. The situation was tearing me apart.

On the Monday, I phoned the solicitor. 'You might have heard that Dave moved back for a while. Well, not any more. He's gone. For ever this time.'

'I've heard that before and nothing changed. You're still there, in my house. We have to make a clean break. I'm still willing to help. You didn't like the house I found, so why don't you go looking for yourself? I'll pay the deposit if necessary. I need that house back and you need somewhere to live. We both win.' I agreed.

I told Alan about the deal I had made. 'I want to move back to Bradley Stoke. It'll be easier for the kids. Will you help me look?'

A fortnight later, we struck gold: a four-bedroom house, five minutes from the school, modern and clean. I put my name down for it immediately and we were accepted. We could move in three weeks.

During that period of house-hunting, Alan and I must have looked at dozens of places. We spent a lot of time together and I was very grateful for his support. He made me feel safe. When he held my hand, it gave me strength. With Dave finally gone for good, I was aware our relationship was changing. I didn't fight it.

Karissa and Ricky were excited about the move. Although they hadn't shown it, they had been affected badly by the rows and were pleased to be getting away. They understood that their father wasn't coming; I was upfront about that. I felt enormous resentment towards Dave. He had hurt me and I held nothing back from the kids. I should have, but I couldn't stop myself. Attempting to force a wedge between the kids and Dave was the answer to nothing, but doing so gave me some satisfaction.

Mum's overriding emotion was relief. She knew the

pressure that we had been under and had experienced at first hand the poisonous atmosphere. Money worries, infidelity and alcohol do not bring peace and tranquillity. She had tried to get Dave and me back together and it had failed. It was time to escape and start again.

Alan and I spent a lot of time together in the run-up to the move. We occasionally went out for a drink or a meal, but more often he was just there, in the house, watching television with us, eating, chatting and laughing. When the kids went off to bed, we would talk. I told him about my plans for setting up my after-school scheme. Over the year since my sacking, I had made good progress, even securing the promise of some funding if I could demonstrate it was a viable proposition. I was certain I could. The research I had undertaken had proved there was huge demand. Alan was very supportive and it was good to talk it through with him. He lived in a one-bedroom flat on his own and he went home every night, even though I didn't always want him to. By the day of the move, we had kissed, nothing more.

I picked up the keys and Alan took a day off work to help. He was fantastic and that evening, with boxes everywhere and almost nothing in the right place, we all celebrated our new beginning with a Chinese takeaway and enthusiastic talk of the future. It was exciting; everything seemed to be coming together. I watched Karissa and Ricky laugh when Alan told stories about me when I was younger. He felt very much part of our life. Was this what I had been looking for all these years? Had I finally found the safe haven from which I could begin my new life?

'Don't go back to your place tonight,' I said to him once everyone else was in bed. 'Stay with me. You're part of this family now. This could be our house, together. What do you think?'

Inside a week, he had moved in. Karissa and Ricky were pleased; they liked having Alan around. Mum was more cautious. 'Are you sure you know what you're doing? Don't you think you should give yourself some time to think? I like Alan – he's a good man – but this is too quick. If it's right now, it'll still be right in six months. Why don't you wait?'

I didn't listen. I was certain I was finally on the correct path to the life I had always wanted. The kids were happy, the house suited us and I was making progress on my business. I had set up a desk with files and a phone and a basic computer and printer. I was taking the first steps in a new world and I was loving it. Success and money were around the corner. The door had been closed on the past and if the memories of disappointments, the guilt and the dread that had sometimes threatened to overpower me tried to push through, help was at hand.

Mum had been suffering from arthritis for a while and had found that distalgesics provided great relief. She had mentioned this to a family friend who had links to the medical profession and she had sent Mum a supply of co-proxamol, as the drug was now known, to keep her going – many more than she required. She put them out of harm's way in a cupboard, out of reach of the kids but not me. It was an Aladdin's cave packed full of hope.

There were enough pills to last me a long time, more than enough, so I began taking them when I didn't need to. Mum had no idea how many she had and didn't miss them. Even the fact that I no longer needed to find excuses and stories for the doctor added to my sense of well-being. That had become a problem, with more and more probing questions being asked each time, but now that pressure was gone. I told myself it was what I deserved.

As they had in the past, the DGs made me physically sick, but I refused to accept that they were doing me harm. They made me feel too good. If I threw up before they had time to get fully into my system, I would take some more and feel increasingly ill. I couldn't hide this cycle for long.

Alan confronted me one afternoon. He had come home early and seen the state I was in. Moments before, I had vomited, and I was pale and shivering. 'You have got to tell me what's going on. I haven't said anything because I know you hate people prying into your life, but it's gone too far. Are you ill? Have you seen a doctor? What's wrong? I'm worrying myself sick.'

He looked so sincere, like he really cared, that I broke down and told him. He was shocked. 'Why do you need them? Nothing bad is going to happen. Not now that we're together.'

I listened to what he was saying and, through the haze, it began to make sense. 'But I'm scared to stop taking them,' I told him. 'I need them to be able to face you, or anyone. I'm nothing without them.'

'That's not true, Laura. It might have been before, but it's not any more. You've got everything you need right here. Me, your mum, Karissa and Ricky. You don't need anything else. You're better than that.'

I realised he was right. That was my old life; this was my new one. That afternoon, I stopped the pills, although I couldn't give up the drink. I needed a few cans in the evenings to help me sleep. Alan had begun to realise how reliant I was on alcohol, but he didn't try to pressurise me to stop. Tackling one addiction was a big enough undertaking.

Almost overnight, I attempted to turn into a domestic goddess. I decided that my mistake in the past had been not creating the ideal home. I began to cook and bake. I wanted delicious smells and big family dinners – pies, soups, cakes, anything I thought a 'proper' mum would make. And when I wasn't in the kitchen, I was at my desk, building the business, proving it was possible to have it all.

For the first time in my life, I told myself, I was equal to my sister. From the day she was born, I had felt she had outshone me. As a kid, she'd looked pretty in her dresses and suits and she would make people laugh; as an adult, she had a successful husband, a lovely house and two adorable children. She had the life I wanted and now, at last, I had it too.

Ashamed

I began to put on weight and told myself it was because I was content. I decided that we had to go on holiday together as a family. Unconsciously, I chose the most appropriate location, the ultimate unreal world – Euro Disney. It was a great success, we had a lovely time, but it wasn't reality. Deep down, I knew that. I wasn't on a par with Dawn. Her life was honest; mine was false.

The house that represented my new start wasn't mine. We weren't even going to be able to stay there for very long. It was only available on a short-term lease. The cooking was an attempt to keep myself from thinking about my pills. My wonderful new relationship was with a man I had known years before and who reminded me of a time in my life when the world was simpler and easier. He was good to me, but he wasn't the man I actually wanted. That was Dave, who didn't want me. I was putting on weight because I was eating too much and still drinking too much. Mum's home-brew wine or bottles of Tia Maria would often follow my cans, giving me dreadful hangovers that stopped me functioning properly in the mornings. I wasn't content and happy; I was self-conscious. My husband had run off with a skinny teenager and all I could do was get fat.

The reality of my life was not slow to catch up with me. It announced itself through first my children and then social services.

'Dad's living on the next street!' Karissa and Ricky shouted in unison as they burst through the front door. 'He asked tons of questions and he says he wants to see us,' they continued excitedly. I couldn't blame them for being happy about it, but I felt sick as they chatted on, explaining what had happened. It was a Saturday morning and they had gone out to the shops. By chance, Dave had seen them. He had been in his car with Tracy and had pulled over. I felt crushed. This was the worst luck imaginable. I had intended to get in touch with Dave at some point, to tell him where we had moved to, but on my own terms, not like this, and I reacted badly, trying everything in my power to stop him seeing his children. Eventually, however, the issue of access was sorted out and I instigated divorce proceedings. Before the end of the year, our marriage was formally another failure in my life. I took no pleasure in that fact.

The one thing that felt real throughout that time was my business, the plans for which were nearing completion. The first step had been to find premises, which proved surprisingly easy. I found a hall set off the road near the school, with toilets, a small kitchen and a safe garden out the back where we could have picnics and set up games. Stage two was securing equipment. I knew I wouldn't be able to afford everything new, not initially anyway, but I was also aware that what I was proposing would be of huge benefit to the local community and I was confident that local businesses would want to become involved.

I had been writing letters, placing adverts and making presentations for some time, promising that all the companies that helped would be fully recognised. The response was excellent. There was a genuine feeling that they wanted my business to succeed. I was offered chairs, tables, desks, kitchenware, games and toys. I even contacted Shepton Mallet prison, where, in return for a small donation, the inmates made me wooden trolleys and cars for the children to play with. The whole process was exhilarating and extremely satisfying.

One of the reasons businesses were willing to help was the response I had received from a number of mailings to local parents. Initially, I canvassed opinion as to whether a new club was something people were interested in. The response was an overwhelming yes. After that, I kept in touch with brief updates on progress, to show that I was fully engaged and organised. When I asked parents to commit, they already felt involved. By the time I was looking for donations, I had 50 families enrolled.

My intention had been to both own and run the play club.

That was my fatal error. I hadn't done my homework properly and it was a hard lesson to learn. When I applied to social services for a licence, I was told that they would have to undertake various checks on me. Fair enough, I thought, there are children involved, but what I hadn't reckoned on was the fact that they would speak to my GP. They were told about the prescription tablets I had been taking and also that there were concerns that I might be suffering from depression following my marriage break-up. The licence would be declined if I was to be in charge day to day but approved if I could find a suitable manager.

This was a blow, but I refused to let it floor me. I advertised and found what seemed to be the ideal person. We opened in the early summer and from day one it was a great success. Parents and children were happy, social services gave us a positive assessment and everything ran smoothly for eight weeks. Then, as we were closing up one evening, I had a disagreement with my manager over pay and she resigned on the spot. Cash flow was always going to be an issue in those early days and I believed we had agreed to be flexible over wages while we established the business. She thought otherwise.

That left me with a big problem. It was the summer holidays and we had to be open the following morning for the kids who were being dropped off. I only had one option as far as I could see. I would have to take charge in the short term and find a new manager as soon as possible. I never got the chance.

Inspectors from social services turned up at 10 a.m. They had been informed that I no longer had an approved manager. I tried to explain that I was only stepping in on a temporary basis, because people were relying on me, but they weren't interested. As far as they were concerned, it was a black-and-white issue. I either had or did not have the relevant documentation. If I didn't, I had to close. They would supervise the club for as long as was necessary for the parents to make alternative arrangements. I was no longer in business. There were no second chances, apparently.

It was devastating. My future was being snatched away. I had invested so much time, energy and effort into the scheme, but, because of what seemed to me to be a bureaucratic whim, it was all for nothing. It felt as though the world was trying to destroy me once again. If no one cared that I was trying to make something of myself, why should I?

Chapter Fourteen
Tell Me What Happened

'What are you doing? For God's sake, Laura, pull yourself together.'

Alan was standing at the front door looking at me. I couldn't speak. I was sitting on the floor of our almost empty house, back against the wall, arms flopped down by my sides, with empty cans of lager at my feet and another, almost finished, held loosely in my hand, the contents dripping onto the carpet.

The lease on my sanctuary, the home from where I'd planned to launch my business empire, had expired and we were moving. Mum, Alan and the kids were, at least; I was too upset to help. I didn't want to leave and when they had driven to our new house with the final load, I pulled out the cans stashed in the cupboard under the sink. I was meant to be checking the meters and preparing to lock up. Instead, I was drinking. Alan was furious, but when he saw the state I was in, he softened.

'Come on, up you get. I'll sort things out here. You get in the car and wait.' Half carrying me, he manoeuvred me out of the front door and into the passenger seat, being careful that I didn't hit my head. Like you see on television, I thought.

I couldn't bear what was happening. I had invested so many hopes in this house – a fresh start, my own business, a traditional family life – and now we were being forced out, moving to somewhere I didn't like. It was another indication of failure.

Our new home was in a nice area of town, but it was run-down and badly equipped. I felt trapped, surrounded by happy families to whom I couldn't relate and who had no desire to engage with me. Out back, there was a family who loved to play basketball in their drive, mum and dad with the kids, shooting the ball into a hoop attached to the garage wall, yelping with laughter and shouting with delight. Across the street was a well-known local footballer whose son had a toy electric car in which he thundered up and down the driveway, his proud, successful parents looking on, broad smiles on their faces and love in their eyes. The dark jealousy in my stomach felt like an animal gnawing away at me.

I was overweight, unemployed and living in a house I didn't own and hated. To make matters worse, every time Karissa and Ricky came back from seeing their father they were full of how well things were going for him and the fun they'd had. There was even talk of Dave and Tracy marrying.

The one thing that made me feel better was alcohol. Drinking was at least something I was good at, until I became a liability, a danger to myself and everyone around me.

Dawn was back working, part-time, and she asked me to look after her daughter, Paris, on the days she was in the office. It was a perfectly normal, understandable request from one sister to another, but I resented it immediately. In my irrational, feeling-hard-done-by state, it meant only one thing: she was rubbing my nose in it. She had a job, I didn't. Her time was more valuable than mine. I had nothing better to do with my days than look after her 18-month-old daughter. I said yes and tried not to show what I actually thought. I needn't have bothered. My actions made my state of mind perfectly clear.

I would start drinking at lunchtime, not knocking it back quite as I did in the evening, but a steady intake throughout the day to help me cope. There was always a can on the go, even when I had Paris with me. It was the only way I could live with being encircled by happy families taunting me, mocking my squalor and unhappiness. I tried to ease off an hour before I had to go and pick up the kids. I didn't want to be reeking at the school gates. But at times the afternoon hours would merge together in a blur and suddenly it would be time to go, with a full, open can in my hand.

On those occasions, if I had a glimmer of self-awareness, I would put down the can, brush my teeth and rush to the school. Unfortunately, the glimmer was sometimes extinguished by the alcohol.

One afternoon when I was running late, I bundled Paris into her buggy, remembering to strap her in, thank God, took a swig of my can and was outside on the street before I noticed I still had it in my hand. Who cares, I thought. I know what I'm doing. There was a holder for a sippy cup by the handle of the buggy. I took Paris's cup out, stuffed it underneath her seat and popped in my can. That was clever.

I finished the lager just before I reached the school. There was hardly anyone there. Why had I panicked? I must be early. Karissa and Ricky were waiting for me. There was a teacher with them. They were the last two kids to be picked up. I staggered round the corner, the buggy swaying back and forth.

Karissa didn't want me getting anywhere near her teacher. 'There's Mum!' she shouted and grabbed Ricky's hand. 'Thanks. Bye.'

I was tired. I wanted to sit down, just for a moment.

'I'll push Paris, Mum. Come on, let's go home.'

I shuffled along behind Karissa and the buggy. Ricky took my hand. I looked down at his big, frightened eyes. I couldn't think of anything to say. I was exhausted. If I could just rest, I'd be fine.

We almost made it home. A couple of hundred yards from the front door there was a telephone box. I tried to focus on it as we approached. I can lean on that, I thought. Shut my eyes for a second or two. I need a breather, a bit of shut-eye. Then I can make the tea.

I missed it by a mile. My knees hit the ground first, tights and skin ripping, then an elbow and the side of my face. I bit my lip. Nothing hurt but I could taste blood in my mouth. Why were they making so much noise? 'Someone help, please! Mum! Mum! Wake up!' All I wanted was to sleep, that was all.

They couldn't move me. I was conscious but not making sense. The kids were terrified and did the only thing they could: they dialled 999 from the phone box. Within minutes, an ambulance arrived. The neighbours must have wondered what the hell was going on: three kids crying, the paramedics trying to help me to my feet, blood on my face and running down my legs.

Karissa told them where we lived and I was taken home, where the paramedics treated my cuts. Karissa knew Dawn's work number and they called her. She was more in a panic than angry when she arrived, worried about Paris. She didn't need to shout. I knew I had crossed a line. I told her it would never happen again. I promised I would stop drinking. I begged to be allowed to continue looking after Paris. That was important to me. I couldn't face another failure. Dawn agreed to give me one last chance and I did manage to keep that promise. I stopped drinking during the day when I had Paris, but that was the extent of it.

Dawn left when Alan came home. After a restless hour trying to sleep off my hangover in a chair, I was up and about by seven, and heading to the shop as usual. Voices were raised, very loudly, when I arrived home. Neither Alan nor Mum could believe I had learned nothing from the afternoon's shameful episode. I shrugged and carried on knocking back my cans. What did I care?

After sustained periods of drinking, my body would periodically have had enough. I would be violently sick all day, unable to even think of eating, my life force draining away. Alan would put me to bed, where I would lie exhausted but unable to sleep, shaking, sweating and repeatedly vomiting. It was nature's attempt to force me to detox and it was dreadful, lasting two or three days.

When I was like that, it seemed to affect Ricky the most. He would cry himself to sleep, thinking that when he woke I would be dead. During the day, he would refuse to go to school, insisting he had to be home in case I needed him. He wouldn't leave my side and there was no way to force him. In the end, I would let him stay.

There was a gentle tap on my bedroom door. It was the afternoon of day two of one of my meltdowns and Ricky was home. 'Mum, how are you feeling? Can I get you anything? Some water?'

I shook my head. The thought of anything, even water, passing my lips made my stomach turn. 'No thanks, love. I'm OK for now.'

'Can I go across the road to the shops? There's no milk in the fridge.'

I hadn't been shopping for days. 'Of course you can, and get some loo roll as well. We're running short. Be careful.' I fell back onto the pillow. The effort of sitting up and thinking had drained me. I must have fallen asleep then. I'm not sure how much time passed, but it was only minutes.

Ricky came thundering up the stairs. 'Mum! They tried to grab me! The men at the shop! They tried to take me away!'

I couldn't work out if this was real. Your worst fears visit you as retribution when you are experiencing detox. Was I dreaming? The white-faced, shaking boy who leaped onto my bed pulled me into the real world. As painful as it was, instinct took over. Someone had tried to take my son.

'Sweetheart, you're OK now. You're safe. Tell me what happened.'

The story came in a rush. Outside the shop, two men had tried to grab him and bundle him into their car. One of them had been wearing sunglasses, he kept saying. He knew that wasn't right because it was cold outside and getting dark. It made him think the men were scary and strange. That may have saved his life. He had taken a step away just before they reached out to grab him.

The police were quick to arrive. I was still in my dressing gown when I opened the door to them. I looked wretched and felt worse. I told them I'd been ill and that Ricky was looking after me. They sat down with him and he described second for second what had happened. He gave them a detailed description of the car and the men, and again at the station, where they taped the interview. I was very proud of him. He stayed calm and did his best to remember as much as possible. The shop was fitted with CCTV and the tape corroborated everything Ricky had said, but the men were never found.

It wasn't until we got home that evening that the reality struck me: none of this would have happened if it hadn't been for me. Ricky should have been at school, not at home with his mother, the drunk. I should be looking after him, not him me. I had very nearly lost a second child. The thought was unbearable. I was ashamed. It could never happen again. I had to stop drinking, and if I was going to do that I needed to have something to replace it.

Since we had moved, I had been unable to banish thoughts of Bridge View from my mind. When I had finally closed that door behind me, I'd been convinced that I'd locked away all the problems accompanying that bungalow. For six months, that had been the case, but from the moment we had moved again I had been miserable and I found it impossible not to compare the wonders of my beautiful home by the water to where I lived now. I got it into my head that ownership of the house should have rightfully been transferred to Dave and me, that we had shaken hands on a deal and that that was enough. I was determined to fight for what I saw as rightfully mine. I approached a solicitor to discuss a possible claim and was welcomed with open arms. That enthusiasm was all I needed. I would be the owner of Bridge View; it was only a matter of time.

I was convinced we were going to win. I refused to countenance defeat and ignored the fact that we hadn't paid for the materials, as originally agreed, or paid any rent during the time we lived there. All that was immaterial as far as I was concerned and I put it out of my mind. If we didn't get the house itself, I was certain we would be awarded a cash sum. That money was going to change my life, I decided, even though neither our solicitor nor our barrister ever gave any indication as to what we might receive. Without that determination, however, I would quickly have returned to drinking.

The case dragged on for a couple of years, with both sides putting forward claims and counterclaims. By the time it drew to an end, I had been forced to open my eyes and accept that another dream was drifting away from me. We were never going to be awarded the house. It was impossible to prove that there had ever been an agreement to transfer ownership and the economic facts did not readily point towards that conclusion. We did succeed to some extent, however; unpaid wages were offset against the rent that the court decided we owed and we received a small settlement. My visions of space and safety and room to grow had been tarnished by disputes and acrimony and assessed by others as being of low value. It summed up my life.

Around the time that I decided to instigate the claim over Bridge View, we received a letter from our landlord. He wanted the house back and was giving us notice on our lease. We were on the move again. It was a hassle, but I welcomed the news. That house represented a dreadful period in my life during which I had brought shame on myself and my family. I had the legal proceedings to sustain me, to keep me off drinking in the quantities I had been, and now I had to find a new place to live.

Mum chose not to join us. She'd had enough of my antics and I agreed that it was probably for the best. If Alan and I were going to make a family life, we had to do it on our own.

Mum applied for and received a bank loan, with which she bought a mobile home. We were initially provided with temporary accommodation by the council and after a few months we were granted a lovely three-bedroom house. This one, definitely, I told myself, is the castle from which I can take on the world. My drinking was relatively under control and, to prove to myself my intention to look forward not back, I enrolled on an access course for probation work at Filton College. Then, in January 1997, just before the start of term, I was involved in a car accident.

It was lunchtime and I was driving to my sister's. The sun was low and bright and I was stationary at a junction, waiting to turn into her road. The sun must have blinded the driver behind me. He smacked into me and the car behind him didn't have time to stop. Although neither had been travelling very fast, the two heavy jolts, one rapidly followed by the other, were frightening and the noise was dreadful.

The middle car had taken the brunt of the damage. It was a write-off, but my car was driveable. We called the police to report the accident and they instructed me to drive the short distance to my sister's and wait for them there. It was all very straightforward. The cause of the accident was clear and not in dispute. The insurance claim should proceed without any hitches.

I thanked them for their time and help and drove off to pick up the kids from school before dropping in on Alan to tell him what had happened. He was worried that I might be injured and not realise it because of the shock. 'You need to go to the doctor tomorrow, first thing, to be sure. You're pumped full of adrenalin right now, which could be masking an injury.'

He was right. By the time I saw the doctor the following day, I was in pain and he immediately identified whiplash. Later, at home, I was explaining the doctor's diagnosis to Alan and he mentioned that I should consider making a compensation claim. 'It might amount to quite a lot of money, Laura. I've seen it before.'

I had the bit between my teeth. I had been hurt through no fault of my own and the more I thought about it, the more money I could see coming my way. All sense of proportion deserted me. I became obsessed, delusional even, about what my injuries were worth.

A week later, I was back with the doctor. The pain and discomfort had spread to my back and, after being examined, I was referred to a physio, whose ministrations did eventually help. I began to assess other ways in which I had been harmed that might increase my claim. Prior to the accident, Karissa had been helping me with a part-time cleaning job, earning her a little extra pocket money. It was only a couple of evenings a week, but that had had to stop because my back was too painful. It might not have been much, but it was still a loss of earnings. As for college, it was too much to deal with. Loss of potential career? The value of my claim was mounting.

I began to experience difficulty sleeping. I was agitated and put it down to the accident. Whenever I shut my eyes, all I could hear was the crunch of metal on metal. I couldn't stop replaying that moment. As the car ploughed into me, it felt as though I was a rag doll abused by a spoiled child. The memory was almost unbearable. I was referred to a psychiatrist, who diagnosed me with a form of post-traumatic stress disorder.

The Bridge View case was plodding along, but by then it was beginning to dawn on me that it wasn't going to end the way I had hoped. This was my chance; it was only fair. I told myself that I was pursuing compensation to secure a better future for my family, but in reality it was the same old story. I was due something, certainly, but nothing like the figure of £100,000 I had allowed to infect my mind. It was a mirage. I wanted a stable, happy life and I was trying to build it on a foundation of sand.

The victim complex I nurtured was damaging enough, but there was a far more debilitating and dangerous consequence of that accident. I was prescribed painkillers. Dihydrocodeine. Thirty milligrams. They were fantastic. It might be the most addictive drug on this earth; certainly that was my experience. When I took them, I was unstoppable. Any slight doubts as to the outcome of my claim were left by the wayside. I wasn't delusional; I was righteous. Such was the power codeine had over me. I had internal happiness. Life was as good as it gets. The only problem was that I forgot about reality.

Chapter Fifteen

He Said He Was Going to Kill Me

I realise now that I rarely took responsibility for my life. I blamed other people, or the system, whenever things went wrong. It was never my fault; I was due a break and I was justified in trying anything to even things up. For years, all any of this resulted in was unhappiness, resentment and deep-rooted shame. It wasn't until I fully took control of myself, stopped pretending and achieved something on my own merits that I finally understood what peace and contentment – and pride – were. In 1997, that realisation was a long way off.

If it wasn't other people or the system that was the problem, it was where I was living. Houses have played a large part in my life or, perhaps more accurately, I have allowed them to play a large part in it. I transferred responsibility to bricks and mortar; the houses became the cause of my ills. If I can just move, I'd think, everything will work out for the best. There are too many memories here. I need a new start. This move will make all the difference. At least this final time it proved true, after many years of turmoil.

'We have to move back to Patchway,' I told Alan. 'That's where we belong, where we'll be happy. The kids' school is there, and your work.'

We had been in our three-bedroom place for almost a year, but since I'd started on the codeine tablets I'd convinced myself that it was only in Patchway that I could make the life I had always wanted. To be fair, Alan agreed it was time for a change. He didn't like the area where we were living.

'A friend of mine lives in a place in Patchway that I think would be perfect for us,' he told me. 'It's a bit of a state, but we can do it up. It's a good size, in a nice street and with a big garden out back. She mentioned she was behind in her rent and desperate to get out. There might be a way to exchange houses, if we take care of her arrears. What do you think?'

Anything was worth a try and we went to see the house. 'A bit of a state' was the understatement of the century. It was close to derelict. But there was something about the place that I liked. It didn't have the glamour of Severn Beach and Bridge View, or the exciting novelty of that first flat that Dave and I had shared, but there was a solidity about it. I could see myself living there. Since then, the walls have seen a lot. Most of it, I am not proud of. But the house felt like home then and it still does today.

We moved in on my 33rd birthday, in August 1997. It took months of hard work to pull the place into shape and I enjoyed every minute of it. It was a big project and that on top of my compensation claim and the ongoing legal proceedings meant I was constantly occupied, with my little friends in blister packs to keep me company. By Christmas, we had the place pretty much as we wanted it; into the New Year, I was lost again.

Bridge View had been settled towards the end of the year and my insurance claim was plodding along slowly. There was little I could do to move it forward. Life wasn't generating any excitement and once the work on the house was finished, although the painkillers helped, I became bored.

It began slowly. I had been drinking heavily in the evenings, which Alan seemed to be used to and accept as normal, but that changed when my habit took hold during the daylight hours. By spring, drinking was almost like a full-time job to me. The kids hated it, Alan hated it, but I couldn't stop myself. Without drink, I was frightened. From my new home, I could see the house where Natasha had died. It seemed to call me and I would find myself standing at the window for long periods of time, unable to resist staring at the front door that Natasha had never returned to. The reality that I was wasting my life would creep into my consciousness or the black guilt over Natasha seep back into my mind, reminding me what a bad mother I had been. But neither of those was strong enough to take on alcohol. My cans won every battle and I loved them for it. I didn't care what anyone else said or did – until Ricky left.

The kids were spending most weekends with their father. I think they were trying to avoid me, because by late spring my drinking was out of control. Almost every night, I was slurring my words, shouting and swearing at the slightest provocation, falling asleep on the sofa and having to be taken to bed. It was impossible to reason with me and no one bothered trying.

It was affecting Ricky worst of all. Karissa loathed my drinking, but she did her best to ignore it, to not be in the room when I tipped over the edge. Ricky found that impossible. He became agitated and uncomfortable, and would either start crying or try to snatch the can from my hand. That made me angry and I would react badly, verbally abusing him, which brought more tears. Alan was left to tidy up the mess as I slumped back on the sofa, indignant and convinced that I had done nothing wrong.

It was one of those beautiful early summer Sundays, cloudless, warm, with a gentle breeze, ideal for having a few drinks in the garden – a few too many. Ricky came back from visiting his dad and he could see the state I was in. He had wanted to tell me about his day, but there was no point. It wasn't even five o'clock.

'Mum, why do you always have to drink? You spoil everything. No one else does it. Dad and Tracy don't get drunk like you do. It's better round there.'

Hearing her name was all it took. I knew he was right. I felt guilt, but I displayed anger. 'Don't you ever fucking mention that bitch's name to me again! You have no right bringing her up in my house. You did it on purpose, didn't you? You wanted to upset me. You're always trying to spoil things for me. You're a spiteful little brat.' I didn't mean it, but I couldn't stop myself.

Ricky burst into tears. 'I hate you! I hate you! I'm not living here any more.'

He meant it. He took his bike and cycled to his father's. I did nothing to try to stop him. I just opened another can.

In the morning, trying to piece together what had happened through the fog of my hangover, I was devastated. I rang Dave and caught him before he headed to work.

'He doesn't want to see you or speak to you,' Dave told me. 'He's not going to school today because he doesn't have his uniform. You need to pack a bag for him and I'll pick it up at lunchtime.'

'You've got to be kidding me! I'm not going to –'

'Don't make things difficult. Just do it. We'll have to sort this out later, but for once think of someone else and not yourself. Pack the bag.'

I didn't have much choice, but I wasn't going to take the situation lying down. I called social services and my solicitor. I gave the impression that Dave was forcing Ricky to stay. The reaction of the authorities was a million miles from when Dad had taken Dawn and me away from Mum. They went straight round to Dave's to find out what was happening. Ricky told them he wanted to stay where he was. That tore me up. I felt sorry for myself. It was Dave's fault, I reasoned. He must have been poisoning Ricky against me. It was nothing to do with me. I drank even more than normal that night, to fight off the truth.

The only winner in the desperately sad situation was the solicitors. They exchanged letters, I applied to the court to force Dave to give Ricky back, but eventually, weeks later, Ricky came home on his own, initially staying in his bed for a night or two a week and then longer until he was back permanently. It was where he belonged, despite his mother's behaviour.

Ricky leaving shocked us all, but when it happened I didn't give up drinking. I didn't want to admit it was my fault until Alan pushed me to confront it.

'Laura, I've left you alone for the past couple of days, to let your rage die down, but now we need to talk. You must make changes or you'll lose your son for ever, and maybe Karissa too. I know you don't want to face this, but you have to. You have a drink problem. You need help.'

He was serious and concerned, holding my hand across the kitchen table, and his words made an impression. I had never acknowledged that I had a problem to myself, let alone anyone else. I am in control of my drinking, not the other way round, I would tell myself. I drink because I enjoy it, not because I have to. Self-delusion is far easier than self-realisation. Sitting there with Alan, I forced myself to confront my addiction, even though it scared the hell out of me.

'I've been speaking to Mum,' Alan continued. 'I had to talk to someone and there was no way to get through to you. I've been out of my mind with worry. If it helps, she says she's happy to go along to the doctor with you, as support. I know it's hard to face up to, but for the sake of the kids, and for yourself, I think you should go.'

His mother came round that evening to discuss my addiction and I agreed to make an appointment with the doctor. I couldn't have faced it on my own, but going with Alan's mum somehow made it seem possible. Could this finally be the start of a liberated existence for me, free of the desperate need to drink and free of the pills? If I was going to defeat my need for alcohol, I was going to try to take on the painkillers at the same time. Before my resolve left me, I collected all the packets I had in the house, emptied out each tablet and threw them in the wheelie bin outside. It felt like a big step forward.

The doctor's appointment was easier than I had anticipated.

The lady we saw that day was very supportive and didn't seem to be judging me. We talked for almost an hour, discussing why I felt the need to drink, how it pushed away all the dark thoughts I had inside about my failures in life and about Natasha. The first few days were going to be the hardest, she explained. The most important thing was that I had to want to help myself. If I did, if I truly had the strength, then she could help. She prescribed Librium tablets, which would help counter the severe withdrawal symptoms, the shaking and the sweats, plus a sedative. As we left, there was one sentence that I couldn't get out of my mind: 'None of this will work unless you really want it to, Laura.' Did I? Yes, desperately, but I wasn't sure I could do it.

The following two days were a nightmare. All I could think about was having a drink. Just one, to settle me. It wouldn't be as though I was drinking properly. I would be weaning myself off gradually. But I knew that wasn't true and I managed to resist, with assistance.

On the morning of my second day without a drink, the smell of it leaking out of my pores, and with barely the energy to put one foot in front of the other, I telephoned my usual GP and begged for a prescription for painkillers. He refused. I suspect he had been expecting such a call. I was left with only one possible course of action. On my hands and knees, I picked out the individual tablets from amongst the potato peelings and discarded leftovers in the household rubbish. I told myself I needed their support. That was true. They did help me over that horrible week. But they also represented a failure, and the failure had felt good. Hard as I tried to convince myself, the reality was that I didn't really want to succeed. I was too weak. It was only a matter of time before I had a drink.

My doctor had realised I was going to require more than withdrawal medication and sedatives if I was going to beat this and he referred me to a drying-out clinic in Clifton, the Robert Smith Unit. The place had an excellent reputation and

I agreed to attend in an attempt to push back that inevitable first slip. I approached the treatment with an open mind, but I couldn't banish a nagging voice in my head: you are only playing at this, Laura, just playing; this isn't you; this isn't serious.

I didn't drink during the period I was going there. I couldn't have continued with the treatment if I had, because they breathalysed you every morning. Clifton was nearby, which meant I was attending as an outpatient. I don't think I could have coped if they'd insisted on me becoming a resident. Being pressured would have pushed me away.

The treatment was a mixture of group therapy and one-on-one counselling. I could see how it was benefiting some of the others there, many of whom were homeless and were also being provided with basic educational skills in order to assist their reintegration into society. I have huge admiration for the work undertaken at the unit, but it didn't quite gel with me. I got very little out of the group sessions. Other people's problems weren't the same as mine and had no bearing on my life. I was unique, I thought, and the sessions weren't getting to the heart of my issues, so why bother? The individual counselling was good, but it wasn't regular enough for me. I wanted more attention and if I wasn't going to get it, I wasn't going to waste my time. I stopped going after two months. It wasn't working for me.

The one thing being treated at the unit had opened my eyes to was the benefit of a regular routine and after I stopped attending I decided to find a job. I had to keep busy if I was to take my mind off alcohol. I began working as a receptionist in the maternity department of a large hospital. It was a good position, with some responsibility. The only problems were that it was afternoons only, which meant I wasn't around when the kids came home from school, and I had to take a bus to get there. Driving was impractical as there was no parking available.

It was a bad decision. My failure to complete the Robert

Smith course had left me more fragile than I realised. I had deluded myself that I had extracted all that was useful from it, but in fact such treatment requires completion to be properly effective. I was vulnerable, and hating the bus journey and missing the kids gave me the excuse I needed. I couldn't be expected to deal with the stress without help.

'It's just the one can, Alan, to help me sleep.' I wasn't kidding anyone. Alan tried his best to stop me, but short of locking me in a room or tying my hands behind my back, there was nothing he could do, except be there to pick up the pieces.

Within a few months of starting the job, I was back drinking full-time, trying desperately to hide the fact from Alan and Ricky. I would ask Karissa and a friend of hers to come with me to the local shop, where I would buy my supply and then beg them to hide the cans up their sleeves as we approached home again, so that Alan couldn't see how many I had. Karissa hated this, but I gave her no choice. I would plead and weep, telling her that this was the only way I could cope and that it was only for the short term. Once smuggled inside, the cans would be stashed in the bathroom washing basket. I would then announce that I was going to take a long bath, which, with the door locked, allowed me peace and privacy to get on with my drinking.

Before starting a shift at the hospital, I would pour lager into a water bottle and drink it on my way there. People were relying on me at work, but I was in no fit state. The more I drank, the more it depressed me. I was a master at hiding the evidence, but I couldn't cover the effect it was having on me. It wasn't long before my manager called me into her office.

'Is something wrong, Laura? You don't look right. Is it the job? Can I help?'

I told her I hadn't been feeling well. I didn't explain why.

'Why don't you take a day or two off, to get back on your feet? We'll cope in the short term without you. Give me a ring when you're on the mend.'

Ashamed

Halfway home, I got off my bus outside an off-licence. It was impossible to resist the urge. The second bus I caught was packed, but I found myself sitting alone, slurping out of my cans. No matter how crowded the passengers are, no one ever wants to share a seat with a drunk, especially in the middle of the day.

I never went back to work. I had failed again, which meant only one thing: more alcohol. Alan's patience was at breaking point, but he tried his best to stick by me. There were moments, such as when Ricky eventually came back home, when I would manage to stop, for a week, perhaps longer, but I always slipped back. Life became a haze and my behaviour increasingly irrational.

I was being followed. I was certain of it. I had noticed the same car outside my house for the past two days and here it was again, right behind me as I drove with a friend to the shops. I had a fair idea who it was. Someone from the insurance company I was in dispute with over my compensation claim. We were nearing the end of the process and both sides were pushing for a settlement to avoid court. My initial dreams of receiving £100,000 had long since disappeared. They had challenged me at every turn, insisting my problems were not as serious as I claimed. I'd been warned this might happen; it was common practice apparently. My solicitor was pushing me to accept the offer they had put on the table. If I didn't, he said, I might end up with nothing. The car behind me was clear evidence that he was correct. I asked my friend to take down the car's registration number in case I needed it.

It was the spring of 1999 and the television presenter Jill Dando had recently been shot. It was a dreadful, horrible incident and had dominated the newspapers for days. That was what must have put it in my head. When I got home, I called Alan at work. 'Alan, come home, quickly, please. I've had a phone call. It was a man. I don't know who. He said he was going to kill me, to shoot me in the head. And someone has been following me.'

Alan took what I said at face value. 'Lock all the doors. Don't open up for anyone but me. I'll be there as soon as I can. Call the police.'

I did and when they arrived they too took my story seriously. I described in great detail the phone call I had supposedly received and gave them the registration number of the car. They gave me a special number to ring and a code word to use if I ever saw the car again or received another phone call. Thank God it fizzled out quite quickly after that. We must have jotted down the registration number incorrectly because the police informed me later that they couldn't trace the car. I settled with the insurance company, so it was no longer necessary for them to follow me and, obviously, I never received 'another' threat.

It was a terrible, selfish thing to do. It wasted police time, caused Alan unnecessary worry and could have resulted in a dreadful experience for the man who had been following me, doing his job. Once again, I had wanted the attention, for something to be happening in my life, to be the centre of everything. I wish there was a better explanation than that, but there isn't. I had ceased to think or function properly.

In August, I went on holiday to Sandy Bay with Dawn and our four kids. We had a good time, perhaps because I wasn't drinking. Dawn had made me promise. But if I wasn't having alcohol, I needed pills. I couldn't live without both. I was terrified I was going to run out until I saw the pharmacy at that campsite. Here was a new audience for my tales of various ailments. I told them I had left my own pills at home. I was quickly provided with the necessary prescription and a happy time was had. Then I arrived home.

The minute I walked through the front door, I knew something had changed. Alan was off with me, colder. It appeared he wasn't happy that I was back, that he had been happier on his own. He had seen a new future, free of me, and he liked it better than the present he was living in. I was sure I wasn't imagining it, although he didn't say anything, and I reacted in the only way I knew how. I went straight down to the local Spar, bought a load of cans and went on a bender. For a week. If he hadn't before, by the Friday he had had enough.

I was pissed when he came home from work. We had agreed to go out and have a proper talk, away from the house. I had totally forgotten. He was so angry he could barely speak. He turned his back on me and went out to the garden to mow the lawn.

In an ill-conceived attempt to make up, I decided to cook him something to eat. I put the bacon under the grill and sat back down in the lounge, waiting for the delicious smell to tell me it was time to turn the rashers. I opened a can and the minutes drifted away from me.

'Laura! Laura! For fuck's sake! The grill's on fire! What are you trying to do? Burn the house down?'

I must have passed out. Alan had smelled the smoke and rushed in just in time to avert a major disaster. Flames had been licking at the front of the stove. It would have been only moments before the kitchen curtains would have caught light. After that, who knows?

'This is the last straw, Laura,' Alan said after he had put out the fire. 'I can't take any more. I've tried to help, I've tried to understand, but you don't want to help yourself. And until you do, there's nothing anyone else can do. You're killing yourself and I can't sit by and watch it any more.'

Alan slept on the sofa for the next few nights, but I still didn't believe he would actually leave. A week later, he announced he had found a flat nearby. On the Saturday, he started to pack his belongings. By that evening, he had gone.

'Laura,' he said as he put the last box in the back of his car, 'I still love you. I will always care for you. But living like this is tearing me apart. I'm sorry. I'm not disappearing out of your life, though. If you need anything, you can always come to me. Try and be strong. You're a better person than you allow yourself to think you are.' He kissed me on the cheek and drove off.

Over the years that followed, he was as good as his word, dropping by from time to time to check we were OK and had enough food and money to live on. We've remained friends to this day.

Chapter Sixteen
I Would Like to Say Goodbye

With Alan gone, what little restraint I had dissolved. I was miserable, sad and lonely. In August 1999, there was tremendous excitement about the solar eclipse. Friends headed off to Newquay and Glastonbury to experience this once-in-a-lifetime occurrence and my kids watched in awe with their special glasses. I remained alone at home, with daytime television, drained of enthusiasm for life. All I cared about was my pills, and getting hold of them was becoming a problem.

My doctor had had enough. There was no excuse that I hadn't tried. They'd been accidentally put in the washing machine, left at my cousin's, stolen from my bag, thrown away by mistake. For a while, I had managed to squeeze additional prescriptions out of him, but not for some time. He was aware of my addiction and was attempting to treat that, not my demands. The only course of action left was to change doctor. With luck, my records would once again take time to catch up with me.

It didn't work. I was too well known in Patchway. 'Please sit down, Laura,' the doctor said on my first visit to the new surgery. 'I must tell you from the outset that I am well aware of your problems. I don't yet know your medical history in depth, but I do know you are addicted to painkillers. I have some experience in this area and I understand how difficult it is. I am here to help. Together, I am sure we can beat this.'

It wasn't what I wanted to hear but I didn't have much

choice. I had to sit and listen. 'We need to put an action plan in place to slowly reduce your intake. Cutting you off completely at this stage isn't feasible.' This sounded promising. 'How many are you taking a day? It's more than eight, isn't it?'

I wasn't going to admit the truth. If I told him I was taking up to 20 a day, usually after starving myself to maximise the hit, I was sure he would insist I be transferred to some sort of rehab clinic. I told him I was taking 12.

'OK. We'll start there. I'll give you a week's prescription, 12 a day. You must promise me you won't go over that limit.'

I promised, although I knew there was little chance I would manage it. It wasn't the outcome I had been hoping for – I was still left with a major supply issue – but at least I had something in the short term. The solution to my problem came from an unexpected source.

With the feeling of abandonment since Alan's departure overpowering me every day, I decided to seek support in family ties. I made contact with Dad again. No matter what had gone on before, there was still the unconditional love that exists between a father and daughter. He would care what was happening to me and fill the void left by no longer having a man in my life.

Dad was delighted when I called and we arranged to meet. He was not in a good way. Loneliness had taken its toll. He had split from his partner and was angry about how we had turned our backs on him. Everything was our fault, none of it his. He was being unreasonable, but I let it wash over me. I didn't have the stomach for a fight. He remained bitter about his perceived ill treatment, and was prone to throwing it back in my face whenever we had cross words, but, as well as venting his frustrations, he also displayed his considerable charm. He was a natural storyteller and loved to exaggerate and spin tales, and I began to enjoy seeing him.

'I've got a secret to tell you,' he said during one visit. 'You have a cousin that I have never told you about. She refuses to speak to me, but I thought it was time you knew the truth.'

I was shocked. I couldn't believe he had kept it quiet for so long. 'Dad, why have you never said anything before? Who is she? Where does she live?' I had a hundred questions.

'You might know her name. It's Liz . . . Liz Hurley.'

That was Dad to a tee. It was total nonsense, but it made me laugh, and I hadn't been doing much of that recently.

I found them in one of his kitchen cupboards. I was looking for sugar to make a cup of tea, and there they were. Boxes and boxes of co-proxamol. They might no longer have been my drug of choice, but in the circumstances I wasn't about to complain. I asked him what they were for.

'I've been suffering for ages with chronic pain in my neck – and it isn't just you,' he laughed. 'I've got a repeat prescription, but I've gone off them. They make me feel sick.'

They did the same to me, but I didn't care. 'Would it be OK if I took a box? I've had these before.' More than you could imagine, I thought. 'They help with my back.'

'Of course, take what you need.'

Happy words to hear. There were hundreds of pills in that cupboard. I was desperate for the release they offered and I would put up with vomiting to get it. I just won't eat, I reasoned. If I have nothing in my stomach, I can't throw up. It'll be fine.

It doesn't work like that, unfortunately. Constantly dry heaving, spitting up bile, is almost worse. The cramps are unbearable and the feeling of the back of your throat being ripped out as you huddle over the toilet, alone and pathetic, is incredibly painful. My weight was plummeting – I was down to seven and a half stone – and my appearance was ragged. To me, it was all worth it.

Christmas 1999 and moving into the new millennium represented a moment of hope for many people, a time to reflect and be inspired by the possibilities of the new age. Not for me. Dad's pills saw me through, and I managed to stay off the drink most of Christmas, for the sake of Karissa and Ricky, but on 31 December I was on my own, lonely and despondent. The kids had offered to stay in, but that would have been unfair. They went to their friends' houses and I watched the festivities on television, let self-pity engulf me, drank my cans and cried. What did I have to look forward to?

Very little was the answer, but at least I kept busy. Dad's supply of co-proxamol eventually dried up, after a furious row over the amount I was taking, which left me with virtually a full-time occupation over the next two years: finding new ways to feed my habit.

The quest consumed almost every waking hour. It was all I thought about. Where can I get more pills? My doctor was of little use, as he was making repeated attempts to reduce my dihydrocodeine intake every two or three weeks, which forced me to become extremely inventive.

I discovered dentists could prescribe. What a fantastic day that was. A whole new arena opened up. I had my script down to a fine art. I was forced far afield because when initially I tried the local surgeries I was recognised and they wrote to my doctor. I had a lot of explaining to do then, turning on the tears when he called me in to discuss the situation. I said I'd genuinely had toothache but was too ashamed to admit that I needed the pills because I thought he would regard it as me letting him down. Absolute rubbish, but I got away with it.

My method was simple. I worked out it was better not to over-elaborate as it was too easy to trip myself up in my eagerness. I would ring up and say I was visiting the area, staying with friends and had horrendous toothache. Not every dentist fell for it, but that was OK. I had a long list, thanks to my well-thumbed Yellow Pages. Some days I could make dozens of calls before I hooked one, and a round trip would take all day, but it was worth it.

I learned to talk as if in pain, which often meant I was able to get hold of the scripts without even being seen. If the dentist insisted I come in, no problem. Sitting in the chair, I would fake dreadful, searing agony as he or she prodded away. I had an abscess in one of my teeth, which had been there for a long time, and that proved a big help. They could see there was a problem and I would pretend it was hurting terribly. It wasn't.

One dentist I called had his phone diverted to home and, after much persuasion, he agreed to see me there. I delivered such a virtuoso performance that not only did he agree to drive to his surgery to write out a prescription, he also gave me some additional painkillers he kept at home in order to provide instant relief from the terrible pain I was suffering. When I called the following week to explain that a burst water pipe had flooded the bathroom cabinet, he obliged a second time.

He mentioned that it was possible to pick up prescriptions from out-of-hours chemists. He probably wanted to make sure I had no need ever to reappear in his life. Pharmacies could sell an emergency supply to tide you over until the doctor's surgery reopened, he explained. Five days' worth, sometimes. Pulling those ones off required even greater finesse. I couldn't just ring up and say I wanted the painkillers; to avoid suspicion, I had to ask for something like an antibiotic as well, so that it looked as if the painkillers were part of a complete treatment.

For these emergency prescriptions, I would give a false name and address, or I would say that I was travelling with my gran and she had forgotten her medication. On those occasions, I was careful to request a list of things that an older person might need, such as Gaviscon or denture cream. A follow-up call the next day often delivered a second dividend. Poor Grandma was in distress; she'd been visiting an old friend and had left her pills behind. Now the friend was off visiting her own family. Was there anything they could do to help?

I knew I was committing fraud, but again I justified it to myself. I wasn't cheating anyone. All I was doing was looking after myself. I did begin to worry that one of the chemists might become suspicious and call the police. This possibility preyed on my mind to such an extent that I stopped watching *Crimewatch*. I didn't want to see myself in the most-wanted gallery.

Such concerns were not entirely figments of my imagination. I always knew there was a greater risk involved in approaching one of the high-street chains. The stores were more likely to talk to each other and there was always the possibility that eventually they would add two and two together and come up with me.

I rang up one such store in Weston-super-Mare early one morning, with my just-visiting story. The pharmacist agreed to my request. On my way over, I called to make sure that the medication had been made up. I always did this, as I didn't want to be waiting in the shop any longer than was necessary. 'No problem at all. It's waiting here for you. Pop in and pick it up.' That was good news and everything sounded perfectly normal.

I arrived and told the pharmacist, 'I'm here to pick up my prescription.' The moment I said it, a door behind the counter opened and two policemen walked out. The pharmacist must have been notified by her head office to be on the lookout for a woman requesting an emergency supply of a specific drug and to inform the police if she received a call.

I was led outside by the two officers. 'We know what you've been doing. This is a warning.' They took my real name and address. 'If you get caught again, you will be arrested. And we're duty-bound to inform your doctor.' I was scared and, to make matters worse, I had no tablets in reserve.

I was visibly shaking as I drove home. The thought of having nothing to take was killing me. Drink wasn't going to be an adequate substitute after the shock I had just received. I knew it was a risk, given that the call from the police would probably have used up the last of my nine lives, but this was an emergency: I called my doctor.

'You need to help me. I've run out.'

He was very angry. 'We'll have to talk about that, Laura. I won't prescribe on request. Especially after what I hear has been happening. Come in and see me later today. I'm going to have a meeting with my partners to discuss your case. Your situation is out of hand and we may be forced to strike you off. I'll let you know when you come in.'

Waiting for my appointment that day was awful. This might be it – no more pills. When I was eventually called in to see the doctor, I tried my best to hold myself together.

'You've obviously got a serious addiction.' I nodded. I was going to agree with everything. I was sure that if I didn't I would be thrown out. 'We've decided to give you one last chance, provided you sign this contract. If you breach the terms, act in a manner contrary to what we have agreed, that's it. We are trying to help you, but if you lie there's nothing we can do. If you break this agreement, you will have to find another GP.'

He gave me a prescription. I was in the chemist next door within seconds.

During those two years, I went through periods of trying to clean myself up. I would follow the doctor's advice for a while, resisting the searing temptation to attempt one of my scams, but eventually I would slip.

The doctor was doing what he could but was faced with a problem. I liked how the pills made me feel. Even on those occasions when I was trying to follow his reduction plan, I never fully embraced it. It was during one of these periods that I was referred to the drug and alcohol dependency unit at Blackberry Hill. I felt the doctor there actually understood what I was feeling. He seemed to be able to see what it was like when I didn't have a constant supply, how it dominated my mind and what I would do to get more. For once, I didn't think I sounded like a freak.

At the end of the session, he decided it was the wrong time for me to be having my prescription reduced. I couldn't believe what I was hearing. Fantastic. He said that I was going to need counselling and treatment but that we had to level out my intake before beginning the reduction. I was back up to an official eight per day. He sent a fax through to my doctor outlining his decision and as soon as I left his office I was round there. I did my best to stick to the agreed dosage, but I don't think I lasted a month before I was back to the Yellow Pages. As for the counselling, I wasn't ready to take that seriously.

It wasn't only the pills I was having trouble staying off. Drink continued to play a part in my life, although less frequently. It tended to be whenever I was running low on tablets and needed something extra. When that happened, I went at it hard. In an attempt to stop these episodes of abuse, I gave AA a try. Standing up, declaring that they have a problem, holding hands, saying the prayer and going through the Twelve Steps works for many people, but not me. I felt that if I was going to benefit from therapy it needed to be tailor-made to my needs. My attendance didn't last long. I realised I was wasting my time and theirs when I left a meeting and went straight to the off-licence.

Emergency prescriptions, phone calls, petrol, alcohol – my addictions were becoming expensive. In desperation, I tried shoplifting, but I wasn't very successful. I was caught in an Asda store. That was bad enough, but to make matters worse Ricky was with me and it was the store in which Mum worked. She was so ashamed she refused to speak to me for weeks.

I'd managed to get away with it a few days earlier, stealing a bottle of Malibu, which I'd drunk on the way home, and I'd decided it was easy. This time, Ricky noticed me slipping the bottle into my bag and desperately tried to persuade me to return it. I ignored him and stormed out of the shop. Security grabbed me before I'd even made it to the car park. I created a terrible scene, trying to claim it was an honest mistake. They didn't believe me but decided not to prosecute, perhaps because of Mum. I was cautioned and sent home.

Did I learn my lesson? No. All I needed was a different

location. I targeted my local shop and was successful on two or three occasions before I was spotted. I had a bottle of wine in my bag when one of the shop assistants chased after me as I left. 'Stop! I know what you've done. I saw you. I know what's in your bag.'

I ignored her and continued walking. If I'd admitted it there and then, the police might not have become involved, but I didn't and they arrived the following day. They'd been shown CCTV footage and it was clear that I'd stolen the bottle. I was taken to the station for questioning and put in a cell.

What should have been a frightening and upsetting situation didn't bother me. The arresting officers were trying to persuade me to seek help, but I wasn't interested in listening. All I wanted was to get out, take some pills and have another drink. This was an inconvenience, nothing more. I was charged and appeared in court, but I did so in a daze. By then, I wasn't living in the real world. I think the judge could see that, and he gave me a conditional discharge on the understanding that I sought help. I knew it was too late.

My financial situation was becoming increasingly desperate and it was clear even to me that shoplifting didn't offer a viable solution. I needed a job and in spring 2002 I found one: admin work in a nursing home. God only knows why they took me on. I had been honest in my application, explaining that I had an addiction problem and that although I was trying to fight it, which was true from time to time, there was still a chance that I would succumb. Hardly the ideal candidate, you would have thought, but they chose to give me a chance.

I was there for two years and during that period I went off on frequent benders, but they couldn't do much about it because they'd been made aware of my problems in advance. I pushed it to the limit. I abused the system and I am not proud of that, but I was caught in a situation that I couldn't control. Without the money from the job, I had no way to pay for my needs. All other considerations seemed irrelevant.

Much of my time at the nursing home was spent on the phone, chasing pills. I was obsessed and often had to enlist the help of others to pick them up for me. I had a network of friends who drove long distances to help me out. If no one was available, then I turned to taxis and would have to borrow money from my workmates to pay the fares when they arrived to drop off the prescriptions.

There was one bright moment during these wasted years. When I worked the early shift, I would be home in time to prepare tea for Karissa and Ricky. They were both still living with me. Karissa was at university studying nursing and Ricky was halfway through a three-year apprenticeship programme for vehicle painting. *Richard & Judy* was on in the kitchen while I was cooking and it was the quiz segment, 'You Say We Pay'. I decided to call in and, incredibly, I was selected. It was brilliant. I won £5,000. I told the kids we would spend the money together, on something special (although when we eventually did, it was a disaster).

Having promised that I wouldn't touch the *Richard & Judy* winnings until we had decided what to do with it, for once I stuck to my commitment, which was all the more surprising considering how short I was of money. My job wasn't well paid, my drug expeditions were taking me further and further away, and I required increasing amounts of pills to provide even a basic hit. I took to grasping any opportunity that arose to get my hands on medication, regardless of what it was. Antidepressants, sleeping tablets, if I thought it would have an effect I would give it a go. On one occasion, I conned a chemist into prescribing a sedative for my cousin on the grounds that we were in the area for her mother's funeral and she was so upset that she couldn't sleep. I took it before I drove home and as the dials on the dashboard began to slip in and out of focus, I was forced to call Karissa with a tale of feeling unwell and ask her to come and pick me up.

* * *

The ringing of the house phone startled me. I was slumped on the sofa, half asleep, having taken the few remaining pills I had, which had not been sufficient to lift me out of my depressed state. I picked it up automatically. It was an old friend.

'Laura, how are you? I haven't heard from you in a while. I hope everything's OK.' I mumbled that I hadn't been very well recently. 'I'm sorry. I won't keep you, but I thought you would want to know, since you're fond of my dad. I'm afraid he's been diagnosed with cancer. He's at home with me. I'm looking after him. But the doctors tell me he hasn't got long.'

I just about managed to say how sorry I was about the news before making my excuses and hanging up. But something had registered and was fighting its way through the muddle of my brain to the surface. Cancer, doctor, home care. Morphine. I pulled myself together and called my friend.

'I was having a dizzy turn and couldn't really speak earlier. That's terrible news about your dad. I appreciate you telling me. I'm sure it wasn't easy. Please give him my very best. Would it be possible to come round? I know it sounds awful, but from what you said I might not get another chance. I would like to say goodbye.'

She seemed to appreciate the apparent kind sentiment and said she thought her father would be pleased to see me. He was fading, but a visit might give him some cheer. I told her I would be round within the hour.

After sitting impatiently with her father and holding his hand as he lay, pale and tiny, propped up in his bed, I said yes to my friend's offer of a cup of tea. I didn't want to drink it, but I needed an excuse to stay longer and look around. There it was on the kitchen table: a bottle containing morphine solution.

As we waited for the kettle to boil and my friend fussed with the tea bags and biscuits, I took my chance.

'I think I heard your dad calling. I'm not sure. It might have come from outside. Shall I go and check?'

I knew she wouldn't say yes. 'I'll go,' she replied.

I took three or four deep swigs from the bottle. With nothing in my stomach, the effect was almost instantaneous. I wasn't concerned about whether the loss would be noticed. My need was too great. It was a disgusting thing to do. The shame will never leave me and I offer an apology now in writing. I quickly drank down my tea, made some excuse about not realising the time and left. I never saw my friend's father again.

Chapter Seventeen
It's Not What You Think

The Queen had her *annus horribilis* in 1992; I had mine in 2004.

It began well. Early in the year, I took another job, which I was able to fit around my shifts at the nursing home. It was with a care agency, undertaking home visits to the elderly and to carers who might need a hand shopping or cleaning, to give them a break. It was worthwhile, well paid and I enjoyed it. And the fringe benefits, I discovered, were made for me.

With two jobs on the go, by night-time I was exhausted and in bed early. I was too busy to drink in excess, but painkillers were still playing a massive part in my life and I wasn't sure how I was going to juggle my frequent excursions to chemists and dentists with my new schedule. Once again, chance threw me a lifeline, this time in the shape of a client whom I'll call Kath.

Kath was suffering from depression. I wasn't meant to visit her because I wasn't sufficiently experienced to deal with any issues that might arise, but her regular helper was off sick and I stepped in on a temporary basis. I liked her immediately. I could see she had been through a rough time and I shared some of my experiences in the hope that it might help her realise she wasn't alone. She admitted that although she was on medication for her illness, she was unable to kick her drug habit. She had a regular supplier. Was I interested?

It didn't take her long to find a source, although it wasn't cheap. I had moved past 20 a day by now and, at £1 a pill, the cost was significant. But it was worth every penny. The supply wasn't constant, but it was regular enough. I would ring Kath when I was running low and, in those early days, it was rare that she couldn't deliver. Plus my GP was still prescribing at the agreed level, so my addiction was being well fed, especially when another supply route opened up.

Many of the people I visited were on medication. They were mainly elderly and forgetful, or suffering from mental problems, so very few of them paid close attention to what they had. It was too much for me to resist.

Mostly, the tablets would be in plain view. When I walked into a house for a visit and saw bottles and packets of interest, my heart would leap. On the odd occasion when Kath was struggling to sort me out, all that was required was to appear unannounced at the front door of one of these unwitting suppliers on the pretext of having left something behind. Once admitted, I would help myself. If anyone noticed the pills were disappearing, it was put down to memory loss or accidentally throwing them away. Once I realised what was possible, I was always on the lookout for more opportunities.

During one visit, I pinched a stash of dihydrocodeine only to discover to my horror that it was slow-releasing. Not what I needed, but I wasn't going to be deterred. First, I tried to release the codeine by grinding the tablets in my mortar and pestle. When that failed, I tried the food mixer, then made an attempt at brewing codeine tea, boiling the tablets until they dissolved. Nothing worked. The house I'd taken those from became one of the few that were safe from my light fingers.

A risky but successful tactic, which I used sparingly, was to call the doctor of a person I visited requesting a repeat prescription on account of a mishap, perhaps the pills having mistakenly been flushed down the loo or the old favourite of their having been accidentally put in the washing machine. Best of all was finding a prescription that had not yet been taken in to the chemist. This wasn't common, but it was almost foolproof. A trip to a distant pharmacy did the trick and I'd adopt a blank look if the missing piece of paper was ever mentioned.

Inevitably, I became complacent. One of my ladies lived on her own near me. She had lost her husband years before and was unsure of herself, but she was not mentally impaired. She had the same pills as my dad, co-proxamol, and I would steal them a strip at a time. It was a Saturday and I had run dry. A weekend without pills was inconceivable. I knocked on the door, shouting through the letter box that I had left my coat. The poor woman didn't know what to do. Her son had given explicit instructions that she should never let anyone in unless the visit was prearranged, but here I was, someone she knew, pleading to be let in. It was dreadful, harassing an elderly widow for my own gain.

I persisted and she eventually gave in. I was full of apologies and pretended to look around for the non-existent coat. Perhaps it was in the kitchen, I suggested. When her back was turned, the pills were in my bag. 'I'm sorry. I was certain it was here. I must have left it somewhere else. Thank you for helping me look. See you next week.' I was off, happy that my weekend had been saved.

Upset, the old lady phoned her son, who came straight over. The son must have been suspicious, because he noticed the missing strip. Within 20 minutes of arriving home, I received a call from my manager.

'You've just been round to see Mrs Reece, haven't you?'

'No.'

'Yes you have. You were seen.'

'Well, whoever said that is mistaken.' I was certain no one could have spotted me and I had to stick to my guns. 'Mrs Reece is confused, that's all. Perhaps someone was trying to sell her something. All I know is it wasn't me.'

It was a close call and the shadow of suspicion was never far from me after that.

In April, I decided the time was right to spend the *Richard*

& *Judy* money. A grand gesture, I told myself, would prove to Karissa and Ricky what a capable mother I was. We went on a skiing holiday.

I didn't put on a pair of skis, let alone go near the slopes. The nearest I ventured to the great outdoors was the walk between the hotel and the local Italian pharmacy. On our first day, I discovered they sold bottles of codeine across the counter, used as drops to suppress coughs. It was expensive but wonderful. I spent all my money and drank them down day after day. It was a million miles away from the cough medicine I was occasionally forced to turn to at home in moments of need. The British medicine contained only traces of the wonder drug, requiring whole bottles to be consumed in a single sitting. I would have to swallow back the vomit trying to drink enough for it to have any effect. In comparison, this was vintage champagne.

I hardly saw the kids. They tried skiing but were miserable. They couldn't communicate with me. If I wasn't high, I was drunk. My routine was simple: sick in the morning because of my hangover, eat nothing, knock back the codeine as soon as I could, drift through the day in a haze, sick again at 6 p.m., raid the minibar at 6.30, crash out at 9.

In some respects, perhaps Karissa and Ricky were lucky I remained in my room for the bulk of the holiday. At least they didn't have to be seen with me in public. I looked dreadful. The years had taken their toll. My skin was grey, my teeth virtually gone, there were clumps of hair missing where I had pulled it out, and what remained was brittle and uncombed. I was thin, not slim. My breath smelled horrible, a result of the acid produced in my stomach by being constantly sick. My eyes were bloodshot and dead.

Somehow, they dragged me onboard the plane home. I have no recollection of it. I was surprised when I found myself in my own bed being gently woken by Karissa. 'Mum,' she said, stroking my forehead, 'I'm worried about you. So I've decided I'm giving up nursing to stay here with you.'

I forced myself to understand what I was hearing. My clever, deserving, hard-working daughter was abandoning her career to look after me. I had promised on the day of her birth to protect her from this and I had let her down. I hadn't quite fallen over the precipice; there was still a trace of self-respect remaining.

'Please, Mum, you have got to stop. Ricky and me, we can't take any more. Please try, for us. We need you.'

Karissa made a massive sacrifice on my account and I did my best not to let her or her brother down. I wanted to stop taking the pills, but I failed. I couldn't see how it was ever going to be possible.

Your body can't ignore years of codeine abuse. It doesn't suddenly agree with your brain that enough is enough and that it is fine to switch off the supply. If only it was that simple. After so long, my body was reacting as if I was attempting to kick a heroin addiction. On our return from holiday, I was in bed for four days. The misery was intolerable.

Every minute dragged; every hour felt like a day. At first, I was looking at my bedside clock incessantly, willing the numbers to move forward. I knew there was a long tunnel of hurt ahead of me and I raged at God's unfairness in slowing down time to drag the horror out. Agitation gave way to pain in every muscle. Vomiting followed quickly, violent and disturbing, ripping out my insides as my body rebelled against the lack of its beloved codeine. I could barely lift my head from the pillow, let alone make it to the bathroom to be sick.

All the time, my children stood by me, wiping the sweat from my face and cleaning up my mess. I couldn't concentrate or make any sense. I rambled and the little sleep I managed was cut short by horrific nightmares: Natasha lonely and crying; my head slipping beneath cold, dark water; watching helplessly as a grotesque creature clawed its way out of my body.

I couldn't take it. No matter how much I willed myself to

climb out on the other side, I knew my body had won. It had punished me by demonstrating how wretched life could be. I didn't crave a drink. I was beyond the thought of putting any liquid in my stomach. But pills . . . My brain gave up the fight. I texted Kath. 'Can we meet?'

Karissa and Ricky were bitterly disappointed. I tried to explain that this was the only way I could make it through. I promised I wouldn't go back to how I had been before. It would be only small dosages, a temporary measure to keep me straight. It was what the doctor would have done, I said, reducing my intake over a period of time until I was clean.

It didn't take long for them to realise I was lying. It was only a matter of days before they were once again living with a mother who was an incoherent wreck.

As awful as it was, and as much as I dreaded it, it was a relief to be back to my old routine. Swallowing the number of pills I was taking each day had become a struggle. I had to employ mental tricks to get them down, convincing myself that the only way possible was with blackcurrant squash. Nothing else would do. It had to be blackcurrant, in one of those small cartons with the straw stuck to the side. Creating a ritual attached some comfort to what had become a harrowing necessity.

Each day was the same. Count out my tablets. Thirty now. Lay them in a row. Pierce the straw through the carton, more often than not with a shaking hand. One slurp. Three pills. Down. Another slurp. Three pills. Down. Halfway along the line, the retching would start.

Both the kids did their best to be with me as much as possible. They were terrified of what I might do when I was on my own. They never condoned my behaviour, but they realised that for now it was impossible to stop it.

Karissa and I had driven to Kath's. She remained in the car when I went inside. The supply had been unreliable in recent weeks and I was agitated and desperate, but I didn't want Kath to see quite how desperate. It wasn't that I thought she might increase the price; I feared that she might cut me off. She was basically a good person who thought she was helping me. If she'd seen how many I was taking, she would have been horrified. The transaction took only seconds and I was quickly back in the car.

Out of sight of Kath's house, I pulled over. I didn't want Karissa to see this, but she had insisted on coming along and I couldn't wait any longer. I opened the car door, swung my feet onto the pavement, placed a road atlas on my lap and counted out my 30 tablets.

The gagging started early. I was hunched over, like an old witch, refusing to turn round as Karissa pleaded with me to stop. The hacking noises I was making were dreadful. I couldn't hold it back. I put my head between my legs and threw up. As I looked down at the pile of vomit at my feet, with splashes up my legs, the white nuggets of relief were clearly visible. I reached down and fished out the slimy pills, some half dissolved. Fighting hard as my brain and stomach protested, I put them back in my mouth and forced myself to swallow, convulsed with violent retches, drool dripping from my chin.

I was sick twice more before we reached home. The final time, in a panic, I tried to scoop up traces of white liquid floating in the vomit. The pills had finally dissolved, as had my last shred of dignity.

With Kath struggling to meet my increased demands, I began to drink even more heavily, with disastrous results. Falling over on my way back from buying my cans became a regular occurrence. Sometimes I would manage to haul myself to my feet and stagger home, other times I would require assistance from a passing neighbour who would half carry me to my front door. It was awful for Karissa and Ricky. Apologising to people who live in your street for the behaviour of your mud-stained, drunken mother is humiliating.

On a rainy day, I slipped and cut myself on broken glass. There was so much blood that an ambulance was called. The gash in my leg panicked me and by the time help arrived I was shrieking as though in agony. The paramedics did their best to calm me down, but I was drunk and confused. On the way to the hospital, their repeated requests for my age and date of birth went unanswered. I couldn't remember, and the harder I tried and failed to force the information to the surface, the more hysterical I became. Eventually, they had to resort to administering gas and air. I was hooked.

A week later, I dialled 999 from home. 'I need an ambulance. It's my back. I can't move. Please come quickly. It's so painful. I'm dying.' Dying for more gas and air. I wasn't very subtle. Back pain or a slipped disc worked well initially; then I claimed to have fainted and cracked my head. On my fourth attempt, complaining of a twisted knee, I was refused pain relief. 'Miss Walsh, we know what you're doing. There's nothing wrong with you. If you continue making these calls, we will be forced to take action.'

They wrote to my GP, who called me in. I was still receiving my regular prescription, now reduced, but we hadn't had a consultation for a few weeks. He was horrified at my appearance. 'How much are you drinking? Are you finding a way to get hold of more pills? I can't help you if you're not honest with me. Will you consider more counselling?'

I lied, of course. It was nothing more than a couple of bad sessions on the drink that had caused the problems. No, I wasn't taking any more pills than he'd prescribed. And yes, I'd have a think about going back to counselling. There wasn't a lot more he could do. I was convincing.

A lady with a Zimmer was the eventual architect of my undoing. She was one of the people on my home-help roster, frail but mentally sharp. She carried around her medication in a clear plastic bag, which she kept on the tray attached to her frame. The first time I went to visit, I could see there was codeine and when I got the chance I pocketed some. On my next visit, in August, I was greedy and took more. She noticed the shortfall and complained. She had initially given me the benefit of the doubt, assuming that she had perhaps mislaid a packet, but twice was too much of a coincidence. The agency rang and accused me of stealing her medication. I was suspended and instructed to come in for a meeting at which they announced they were letting me go.

A month later, I received a call from my union rep at the nursing home. 'Laura, there have been reports of allegations made against you. I don't have all the details, but I have been instructed to tell you not to return to work. You are to attend a hearing next week at which the matter will be discussed. Someone from the union will be there to assist.'

I had no idea what he was talking about. What allegations? I had done nothing wrong. Waiting for that hearing was hell. If I lost that job as well, how would I survive? It didn't matter that I hated it; I needed the money. No money, no pills, no life.

I arrived at head office on the appointed day and learned what had happened. My previous employers, the care agency, had reported me to an authority for the protection of vulnerable adults and children, which was looking into the matter. At the same time, they had taken it on themselves to inform the nursing home of the investigation and the circumstances under which I had been sacked. It was a massive shock. I couldn't understand what was going on and denied all allegations.

I was suspended on full pay pending further enquiries. I heard nothing more until I received a letter six weeks later. For the second time in a year, I was being 'let go'. Apparently, the ongoing investigation into my activities while working as a home help made it impossible for me to continue in my role at the nursing home because of my access to patients. As there were no other suitable vacancies, they had to end my employment.

I was devastated. My world was crumbling around me and I was unable to stop it. I sought sanctuary in oblivion.

* * *

I had been in bed all morning, head thumping from my hangover. I was out of pills and waiting for Kath to call. I had no reason to get up until she did, but the phone refused to ring. I could feel myself beginning to tremble. There was some lager in the kitchen, which would help while I waited. Without bothering to put clothes on, I grabbed the cans, took them back to bed and started drinking. I hadn't eaten the previous day and, as the empty cans began to pile up by my bedside, the alcohol hit me hard. The room was spinning and there were flashes of pain shooting through my skull. I need more drink, I thought. I need more drink. Then Kath will call. That was all I could think about. I went to the shop.

They had seen me in some dreadful states over recent months, but never this bad. I had one thing only on my mind, the desperate need for alcohol, and in my zombie-like state I had walked to the shop naked. The shopkeeper grabbed a blanket as I stumbled in for my cans and wrapped it around me. 'Laura, you don't know what you're doing. Look at the mess you're in. And you've hurt yourself.' There was blood dripping down my leg. I hadn't registered that I was on the first day of my period.

By the end of November, I was penniless. The cost of a tablet from Kath had risen to £2, I was drinking huge amounts of lager and I had taken to calling taxis to get it for me. I was beyond hope.

'Ricky, I'm sorry, love, but I need to borrow some money. I know I shouldn't ask, but I'm skint. I'll repay you when I'm back on my feet.'

'You know I'll do anything for you, Mum. You mean everything to me. I'll lend you the money, of course I will. But you have to tell me the truth. Are you going to buy those pills with it? Because if you take the money, and that's what it's for, well, that means you care more about those tablets than you do about me. Which is it? The pills or me?'

I gave him my answer when I reached my hand out and

took the notes he was offering. I was nearing the bottom of the pit, but I hadn't quite reached it.

I received a windfall at the beginning of December, a £1,500 tax rebate because I'd been on an emergency tax code all the time I'd been working at the nursing home and for the care agency. If the money was to be put to positive use, I had to act quickly. If I didn't, it would soon be screaming at me to buy pills and there would be no hope of resisting.

I repaid Ricky, ordered a turkey for Christmas and bought presents. I even remembered boxes of chocolates and crackers so we could have fun on Christmas Day. But I kept enough aside for myself to make sure Santa Kath brought me the only parcels I cared about.

I called Kath to place an order, a big festive one, and she told me she was expecting a delivery by lunchtime. At one o'clock sharp, I was on her doorstep. 'They didn't arrive,' she said. 'I'm sorry. It's happened before. There's nothing we can do about it for now. Don't worry, I'm sure I'll be able to get hold of some more in a day or so. I'll let you know. But listen, I've got a present for you. This'll help. Hold out your hand.' She placed a small bag of white powder on my palm. 'It's speed. Go home and try it. You put a little on your tongue and let it dissolve.'

I followed her instructions. The impact was astonishing. The need for my codeine pills vanished. I felt alert, buzzing. It was exciting. In that sudden burst, I was interested in everything around me. Television was fascinating, the outside world vibrant and pulsating. When the edge slowly began to blunt, I took some more. And again. And again.

By midnight, a monster lurked in every shadowy corner. The voice on the radio was talking about me. They were searching for Laura Walsh. Someone was trying to poison me. The police were battering on the front door. There was no escape.

I am a drug user. I am going to prison. Someone is behind me. I can't turn around. My brain was flooded with paranoia and the more I panicked, the faster my heart raced. I was sure I could see it thumping beneath my shirt. My forehead was clammy. The hands of the clock began to slow down. Oh no, please, no. I can't face that again. I was convinced I was going into detox. The only thing that could save me now was my pills.

It was an awful night. Sleep was impossible. I was banging on her door at 8 a.m., but Kath had nothing for me. I was burning up and in need of immediate help. There was only one option available. I called my doctor and, for the first time in many years, I told him the truth – almost the truth. I said I had taken the speed by accident. It took ten minutes of desperate pleading before he reluctantly agreed to help. 'I'll give you a prescription for a small supply, but you need to make an appointment to see me on Friday.' I would have said yes to anything. I made the appointment, but I had no intention of keeping it.

Kath insisted on driving me to the doctor's. 'I don't know how you managed to make it over to mine without an accident. You're in no fit state to be behind the wheel. Give me the keys.' I leaped out of the car as soon as we arrived. 'Pick me up one of those little cartons of Ribena and meet me back here,' I called to Kath as I slammed the door shut.

She was waiting for me when I returned. I grabbed the juice out of her hand and began washing down handfuls of pills. There was no time for my ritual. Calmness flooded through me. I turned to say something to Kath and she was looking at me in disbelief. 'I . . . I had no idea,' she stammered. 'So many at once. Laura, you're going to die if you keep taking them. I don't want that on my conscience. This has got to end, now.'

When I called her a few days later to place my order, she was adamant. 'I meant what I said, Laura. I thought I was helping a friend, giving her a boost to help her through the day. But that, that was something different. I don't want any part of it.'

'It's not what you think. It was the speed. Honestly. I only need enough to see me through the holidays, that's all. I can't manage without help. After that, I'm determined I'm going to give them up. You won't have to worry then.' I meant it. I told myself this Christmas was going to be my last as an addict. Whatever it took, in January I would clean myself up, although I had no clear plan as to how I was going to achieve it. But having that goal for the New Year made getting hold of the pills from Kath now completely acceptable and reasonable. In my mind, anyway.

'OK, for the holidays. Then that's it. No more.'

What she gave me wasn't going to be enough. Where previously 30 had seen me through a day, recently the buzz had begun to wear off more quickly. I had tried to stop the numbers creeping up, but it was too hard. I would just have to think of a clever way to talk her round again before Christmas.

I never saw or spoke to her again. On 22 December, with only a couple of days' supply left, I called repeatedly. She didn't answer and I received no reply to my texts. I was on my own.

Chapter Eighteen
I Swear on My Children's Lives

I can remember nothing about Christmas Day or Boxing Day. Christmas Eve found me thrashing through every cupboard in the house in the vain hope that I had hidden a stash of pills somewhere and forgotten about it. I hadn't. I was clean out. I started drinking that night and didn't stop for two days. Karissa tells me she and Ricky made Christmas dinner. I have no recollection.

The morning of 27 December 2004. It is the beginning of the end, although no one knows it at the time. Karissa knocks quietly and gently pushes open my bedroom door. I am lying in my own vomit and urine. With one hand covering her mouth, she tries to shake me awake. My eyes flutter open, but I can't move or speak. It is a scene no daughter should ever have to witness. Things have gone too far. She needs help. Downstairs, she calls my brother Kevin. He lives in Bath and will be there within the hour. She then manhandles me to the bathroom and into the shower. I am conscious but making no sense. The bedclothes are bundled into black bin bags and left outside, too soiled to be used again.

When Kevin arrives, I am lying on the sofa. I pretend to be asleep. I can't face him. Karissa tells him about all the pills, where I am getting them from, how I take them, how long it has been going on. They are talking quietly, but I can hear them.

'You need to make an appointment with her doctor,' Kevin

says. 'Take the first one you can get, let me know when it is and I'll come up. Let her sleep as much as possible and try to get her to drink some water and eat something if possible. It won't be easy, I know. And keep her away from drink if you can. Here's some money for food. Take it. I can see Laura hasn't done any shopping for a while. A hundred quid should be enough to stock up for a few days.'

I was too ill to contemplate drinking that day. I slept for most of it. I sipped at the water Karissa and Ricky brought me, but I couldn't eat. I got up in the evening of the 28th. My arms and legs were aching, I was shivering and there was a fuzziness in my head. I needed a drink. Badly. I needed it like I needed air.

Karissa was working part-time in a local bar and Ricky was visiting his father. They had come in to see me before they left. 'Mum, you frightened us yesterday,' Karissa said. 'It was horrible. If it hadn't been for Uncle Kevin, we wouldn't have known what to do. You remember he was here? He said we should make an appointment with your doctor. He's on holiday this week, but we got the first one after he gets back. Uncle Kevin will take you. We've got to go now, but here's a bottle of water and there's soup downstairs in a pot. You can heat that up if you feel hungry. And, Mum, please don't be angry, but we've thrown out all the drink and I've got your keys and cash. It's for the best. You can't go out tonight. You need rest.'

The remnants of Christmas were still evident in the house when I made it downstairs. The tree with unopened presents beneath it, a pile of crackers on the kitchen counter. No one had been in the mood to pull them. I checked and the kids had cleared out what booze there was in the house, but they'd overlooked something. One of the treats I'd bought with the tax money, for our fun Christmas, had been a box of chocolate liqueurs, the ones that come in the shape of little bottles, with brand labels on them. I snapped the top off each one, poured the contents into a glass and knocked it back. It wasn't enough, but it might clear my head for a while. I sat down to think. Where the hell could I get something to drink? I had no money, no car keys and no way out. Unless . . .

I could make it. It wouldn't be easy, but I was small enough to squeeze through the window in the living room. The larger windows were all locked, but not this one. My destination was obvious. I needed somebody nearby, a friendly face and an alcoholic: Mum's sister Sonia.

I knocked on her door and her husband, Andy, answered. I put on a brilliant act of looking and feeling OK. 'Merry Christmas, Andy. I thought I'd pop over and say hello, have a Christmas drink with you.'

'Sonia, look. Laura's here. Come in, come in. What can I get you?'

Sonia asked Andy to go up to the shops and pick up some cans of my strong lager. I blacked out on their sofa 45 minutes after he returned. I must have had enough alcohol still in my system that all I was doing was topping it up. They tried to wake me, but there was no response. I was out cold. Andy worked himself into a state, convincing himself that I was bound to be sick and choke to death. He rolled me into the recovery position and called an ambulance. By the time they had checked me over and brought me home, Karissa was there, more relieved than angry when I was brought in and put to bed.

The following day, I was back at Sonia's. When I'd woken up in the morning, I'd insisted that my house keys were returned. I had to go and apologise for my behaviour, I explained. The kids realised they couldn't keep me locked up, but they made me promise I wouldn't have anything to drink. I agreed, but in reality that was all I was thinking about. When you are an alcoholic, you become expert at spotting potential sources of drink. It is the one thing you are attuned to. You develop a sixth sense. While I could remember almost nothing about my visit the previous day, one image was lodged firmly in my memory: Andy's bottle of rum on the sideboard.

When I asked for a glass to warm me up, they refused. 'No, Laura, we can't. Not after yesterday. We had no idea things had reached that stage with you. We won't encourage it.'

Then I asked to borrow some cash. I still didn't have my purse. Again, they refused. 'We know what you want it for. You need help.'

I became angry. I needed that rum or I needed some money. They had no right to stop me. As I was remonstrating with Andy, Sonia phoned Mum and asked her to come round straight away. That only added to the sense of injustice I felt.

I had fallen out with Mum and Dawn around the time Alan had left. Dawn had come to the house to pick up Karissa, who was going over to babysit for Dawn's kids. It was during one of my very worst sustained bouts of drinking, and I was tearful and drunk as Karissa opened the front door to go and get in Dawn's car. 'Karissa, love,' I mumbled, 'I need Dawn. I've got to speak to her. She's my sister and I need her. I want to hug her. Ask her to come in. Please, love.'

When I heard the car drive off without Dawn appearing, something snapped inside me. The cow is too goody-goody to step inside my house, I thought. She's always thought she's better than me. Well, I'm not having it.

I called her the next day and we had a blazing row. I told her she was a selfish bitch, that she was neglecting me and the kids and that if it had been her who needed me I'd have been there in an instant. Dawn fought back. 'What crap! You never think of anyone but yourself. I'm not setting foot in a house that stinks of pee just to be sworn at by a drunk! Never ring this house again!'

The anger inside me was boiling over. My family were rejecting me. I thought about Mum. She hardly ever came round either now. She probably felt exactly the same as Dawn. I rang her next, calling her every name under the sun, claiming she didn't care about me or her grandchildren. I was vicious and told her I could get on with my life perfectly well without her.

I hadn't spoken to either of them since and suddenly here was Mum lecturing me, all holier-than-thou. I was infuriated. No amount of trying to talk sense into me had any effect. It was as if my brain was shrinking through lack of alcohol. I couldn't think straight. Reason had no hope. There was only a tiny portion of my mind functioning and it was screaming for alcohol. If it wasn't going to be fed what it wanted, it would reach out for some other form of release: alcohol or oblivion, alcohol or oblivion.

'You can fuck off, the lot of you!' I shouted as I stormed out. 'You don't care about me. No one does. There's no fucking point any more. I'm better off dead!'

I wandered the streets of Patchway aimlessly but found no comfort in the familiar sights. It wasn't home; it was an alien landscape. I found myself at what is known locally as 'the Banana Bridge', a pedestrian crossing over the M5 leading into some woods. It was dark and deserted.

I stood at the apex, looking down at the cars rushing past below. All those people with somewhere to go, unlike me. I was lost. My mind began to play tricks. What is the point? Mum didn't care, she had only come to gloat. Dave was gone. Alan was gone. Dawn could have all the attention she wanted if I wasn't around. And the kids? All I ever did was bring shame on them.

All you need to do is climb over and it will all go away, the darkness inside me whispered. If they won't let you drink, you know what that means. You won't survive that again. Do it. It's simple.

I put one foot on the railing.

There was no one around, but I heard a voice. My guardian angel? I don't know. Perhaps. Whatever it was, it forced its way through the veil that was shrouding my senses. You have options, it said. They are not easy. You have to face yourself. Jumping isn't the answer. Go home to your children. They need you.

I stepped back down.

Sonia or Mum must have called the authorities. They were out looking for me. I turned the corner into my street and saw a police van outside the house. As I approached, they recognised me. They had been issued with a description. 'Laura, you need to come with us for a chat.'

'But I want to go home.'

'All in good time. Come with us for now. It's for your own safety.' They were trying to usher me towards the van.

'I want to go home! I'm all right. I'm all right!'

'Please come with us. You need help. We'll let Karissa and Ricky know you're OK.'

I had to go with them. I later found out that they had been told everything about me – the blackouts, the mood swings, the drinking. And now this: a threat to commit suicide, as they saw it. From their point of view, I needed to be assessed and perhaps admitted to a secure institution – sectioned, in other words.

They booked me in at the station and my belt and shoelaces were removed before I was put in a cell. I sat confused on the bench as the sliding window in the door was opened every few minutes. Suicide watch. I asked why I was being kept there and was informed that a doctor was on his way to see me. I had to be patient. I realised that I had to put on the act of my life or my next night's sleep was going to be in the psychiatric wing of a hospital. I was beginning to shake and sweat. I was struggling to think. I knew I was fast approaching the horrors of detox. I had to fight it off for a little longer.

After what seemed like hours, the doctor arrived. 'I understand you made an attempt to take your life today.'

'It wasn't like that. I was just angry and annoyed at my mum. I've been drinking a bit too much recently and I wanted to lash out, make a point. That's all. I never wanted to kill myself. I've got two kids. I love them. Why would I kill myself? I'm sorry for the fuss I've caused, but this is an overreaction.' I'd rehearsed my speech while I was waiting. It came out in a rush.

He went on to ask a series of questions to gauge my state of mind. My answers apparently satisfied him. 'In my opinion, you are not a danger to yourself. I'm going to recommend that you be released. I'll be writing to your GP suggesting a course of action to help you.'

Kevin was waiting for me when I was signed out. Karissa had called him and he had made the trip over to see what he could do to help.

'Laura, I've got to go,' he said to me, having seen me safely into bed, 'but I'll be back to take you to the doctor. Please try and keep yourself together until then.'

I didn't. I felt dreadful, having had nothing to drink all day. Lying there in the middle of the night, I couldn't face the thought of what was to come. The kids were in their beds. They would be sound asleep. I forced myself to get up and sneak downstairs. I found my purse in Karissa's bag. There was cash in it. Now all I had to do was make it through until the shops opened.

The next two days were worse than Christmas. I drank, passed out, woke up and drank again. Karissa and Ricky could only watch over the carnage and be there should anything terrible happen.

On New Year's Day, my body began its revenge. I had been sick all night and lying in bed that morning I could barely lift my head, let alone contemplate anything passing my lips. I lay in a semi-comatose state as the world tried to push its way into my consciousness. I strained to hear the television in Ricky's bedroom. I tried to focus. What were they saying? It was a report from South East Asia. Something about a tidal wave on Boxing Day killing hundreds of thousands of people. It was the first I'd heard of the tsunami and as I listened I felt ashamed. One of the world's worst natural disasters had occurred a week ago, with devastating consequences, and I had missed it entirely, caught up in my own pathetic struggles. How could you, Laura? How could you? Mothers lost their children, babies became orphans in an instant, while you were lying around drunk and pathetic.

Two days later, Kevin arrived to take me to the doctor's. I couldn't dress myself. Karissa helped as best she could, but I still looked like a tramp. I couldn't bear the thought of being touched. I refused to let her comb my hair. I could only cope with loose-fitting clothes; anything else felt as though it was strangling me.

The appointment was at 10 a.m. Kevin sat with me, explaining to the doctor everything that Karissa had told him. I stayed silent, shivering, trying to hold myself together. The walls were closing in on me and hands were reaching out to grab me, to pull me under the dark, cold water of my nightmares. I was too weak to resist. I wanted to give in.

Kevin was speaking to the doctor: 'I know you were trying to help, to manage her addiction and slowly reduce her dependency, but it hasn't worked.'

'We've been doing our best, Mr Walsh. You have to understand, your sister is very manipulative.'

'I accept that, but what we need now is a new plan, going forward. Look at her. She's a wreck.'

They both turned in my direction. It startled me. I could think of only one thing to say: 'I've run out of tablets.'

'We can't continue prescribing now, Laura,' said my doctor. 'Not after what I've heard today and after this letter I've received from the police doctor. You must see that.'

'You can't just switch me off. It'll kill me.'

'We have to manage both your problems at the same time. If it doesn't work this time, we may have to take other action. It would be a last resort, but we are almost there. We may have to hospitalise you.'

'I won't go.'

'It may not be your choice. I'll be checking in on a regular basis to monitor your progress. But one step at a time. You have to beat the drinking. I'm going to prescribe medication that will help with the withdrawal and a tranquilliser to relax you, similar to what you had before. As for the codeine, I can give you a substitute. It's called Subutex and it works alongside the detox treatment.' The doctor explained exactly how the medication should be administered and Kevin took detailed notes for Karissa and Ricky.

'Finally,' he continued, 'I'm going to refer you back to Blackberry Hill. It is essential that you complete the sessions this time. Let me make this clear: if you lapse, the consequences could be fatal.'

I find it hard to describe the next four days. 'Hellish' is an inadequate word. I'd been through detox before, but never like this. Death had never previously brushed my cheek.

I could keep nothing down, not even water. I was floating in and out of consciousness. If I sat up, my blood drained away and I passed out. Lying down was unbearable, standing impossible. I could feel life trying to float away and I couldn't catch it. I craved alcohol, but the thought made me sick. I knew I was dying and I was frightened. And the nightmares. They were vivid and horrible. In one, I was waiting for Mum to come and take me to the doctor. She arrived with a man I didn't know and I had fallen out of bed, naked. She kept shouting at me, 'Get up! Get up!', but I had lost all power to move. I lay there with them looking at me. The humiliation was horrendous.

Then something in my brain rebelled. I heard a voice. Although I couldn't focus or communicate, there was a scrap of life force left and it kept telling me to breathe. That was all I had left to save me. Keep breathing, Laura. Keep breathing.

For the next two days, I was on the brink, but I pulled through. I kept breathing. The battle was won, but if I was to survive I had to win the war. One more drink would land me right back where I was before, and there would be no second chances then. I had to find a way to be strong.

Lying there, still suffering terribly, a shadow of the woman I had hoped to be, I heard the voice again. Giving life to Karissa and Ricky is the only truly wonderful thing you have achieved, Laura, and you let them down by poisoning yourself. What will happen if you die? Would they blame themselves? Will your legacy be guilt? You know what a destructive emotion that is. Natasha taught you. How could you be selfish enough to allow that to happen? For the first time in your life, show courage. Have a future. Commit yourself to it.

I answered. I swear on my children's lives, I will never drink again. Whenever I feel weak, I will think of Karissa and Ricky. They will guide me through. I owe it to them. I have stolen their childhood. The promises I made before have been broken. I won't fail them again.

Karissa and Ricky represented the one thing I could hang on to: hope.

Chapter Nineteen

I Can Never Go Back There Again

I am sitting on a hard, plastic chair in a small room in the drug and alcohol dependency unit at Blackberry Hill. Opposite me, across the table, is my counsellor, Raj. He's sitting on a similar chair and there is a panic button by his right hand. He is telling me a story about his children and we are laughing. It wasn't like this six months ago.

I hated the place when I first arrived. My doctor's referral had taken four weeks. I resented the wait. To me, it was an indication that they weren't making me a priority. Before my first appointment, my defences weren't merely raised, they were sky high.

I had agreed to attend the unit three days per week for six months. During this period, my medical care was transferred from my doctor to the unit, leaving them responsible for prescribing my Subutex. 'We'll provide a sufficient amount to see you through to your next visit, but only after you pass a urine test each time,' they told me. I thought it was disgusting. They were treating me like a heroin junkie. Then there was Raj. I hated him too. In my eyes, he treated me like a child, telling me what I should do all the time. I deserved more respect.

My attitude was born purely of frustration and shame. I was not in control of my own life and I rebelled against it. What could they teach me? I was smarter than them.

On my first meeting with Raj, he asked me to complete an evaluation form, so that they could assess the state of my mind and the level of depression. The strength of Subutex I would be prescribed would depend on the answers I gave. No problem for me. I would be on maximum in no time at all. The assessment consisted of twenty questions for which you had to give an answer ranging from one to five, with five being the most extreme. I scored five for all twenty questions. Raj, of course, was not deceived. The fact that I had tried it on probably gave him all the information he required about my mentality.

During that session, Raj also asked about my plans for the future. When I replied, 'I'm starting my own business,' I was sure I could see in his eyes what he was thinking. 'Shouldn't you set your sights at a more realistic level?' The most he'd expected of me was the Twelve Steps and attending AA. I was furious and I carried that with me for the following two sessions, offering only antagonism and belligerence. I demanded he increase the strength of the Subutex I was receiving, calling him an idiot for not understanding my needs. I turned up with printouts from the Internet backing up my claims that they were making a mistake and grasped every opportunity to tell Raj he didn't have a clue what he was doing.

He took it all in his stride. He was a professional. On my fourth visit, he sat me down and said, 'Right, I think we'd better start again. We are not getting on. You're working against me, not with me.'

It struck a chord. I had respect for the fact that he'd confronted me. It was as if he actually cared what happened. I let my guard down and we began to build a rapport, although I almost threw it all away by pulling a stupid stunt that was more about testing myself than anything else. I decided I wanted painkillers back in my life.

It would be simple. All that was required was to change doctors again and tell my new GP that I was already taking them. I made an appointment with a surgery nearby and gave them my maiden name, Walsh. I saw an older, female doctor and explained that I was in need of an emergency prescription for dihydrocodeine and was registering there because I had recently moved to the area. She enquired whether I had tried alternative medication and I said yes but that this was the only effective one for my chronic back problem. She wrote me a prescription for ten tablets.

Back home, with the pills in my hand, I experienced a moment of doubt. Why the hell was I going back down this road? It passed and I swallowed them all. I waited for the rush, but nothing happened. Of course, I thought, Subutex contains a blocking agent. That's easy to fix. I'll stop taking it whenever I need a hit. I wasn't bothered about any of this showing up in my urine samples. I felt I could easily justify my actions, saying I'd taken the pills for relief from my dreadful backache.

I returned to the surgery a couple of days later, before my next session with Raj, and was informed I would be seeing a different doctor. 'Miss Walsh,' she said as I began my well-practised spiel, 'let me interrupt you there. I have your full medical notes here. They arrived this morning. I will not be prescribing any codeine-based medication. If you are here to discuss an unrelated ailment, then of course I am happy to listen.'

I discovered later, from Raj, that I had been recognised. A member of staff at the new surgery was married to a doctor at my previous health centre. When it was discovered that I was attempting to register as someone new to the area, alarm bells had rung and my notes had been requested immediately. I wasn't as clever as I thought. I shouldn't have been surprised.

'Mum, you promised! You've been doing so well. Why now?'

I was home and Ricky was angry. I tried to act innocent.

'What are you talking about, love? What's wrong?'

'Listen to this.' He pressed the message button on the answer machine.

'Laura, it's Raj. You need to come and see me first thing in the morning. I've had a call from your new doctor.' The sarcasm was heavy as he spoke the words. 'It appears you have been after pills again. We have to talk.'

The following morning, I had worked out a plan. I was going to turn everything on its head.

Raj was disappointed in me. 'You purposely changed your doctor, you changed your name, just to get pills.'

'That's not fair.' I had my response mapped out. 'One, I've been using Walsh as my name in certain circumstances for a while now. Check my bank details if you don't believe me. I wasn't being false. And two, I was in pain. I needed help. I can't believe you thought I was trying to cheat. How dare you accuse me of that? Do you think so little of me?'

It seemed to work. He said he would ring the surgery and let them know I hadn't been trying to defraud them. 'They may agree to keep you on. I don't know.'

They did and I've been there ever since. I didn't get any more pills, of course, but that wasn't a problem. I didn't want any. Although I tried to save face with Raj by playing the guilt card, the truth was it was me who felt guilty. I had let myself down, I had let down Karissa and Ricky, and Raj, but in many ways I am glad of that lapse. If it hadn't happened, I would still be wondering every day whether a couple of pills might make me sparkle, become more persuasive, better at my job. Now the temptation is gone for ever. I know I don't need them.

I'm not sure Raj really fell for my protestations of innocence. He was an experienced counsellor and had no doubt seen it all before. I think perhaps he understood that I'd had to test my resolve. I had taken one bite of the cherry and discovered I didn't need a second. After that, we got on like a house on fire. In the end, we would talk about life, dreams and hopes. We'd become equals.

The sessions with Raj proved extremely beneficial. As the trust between us grew, I set the agenda of issues I wanted to discuss. From there, through a mixture of coaxing and direct questioning, he steered me towards the acceptance that I had let my life get out of control. Previously, I had convinced myself that whenever I chose to drink or take pills it was because I wanted to, that I had been in charge of those decisions. I began to understand that that was nonsense. The addictions were in control of me and I had to break them if I was to live the life I wanted. It sounds simple, but, having lived so long in a mire of self-delusion, it was an important revelation for me.

It is our last session. We are sitting on those plastic seats and we are nearing the end of my final hour with him. A lot has happened to me in the past six months, important, life-changing events. Raj has helped and I thank him. I won't be back.

'Good luck, Laura. I hope it all goes well. Just one thing before you leave. We've covered a lot of ground in the time you've been coming here – your hopes, your failures, the people you have let down. But we haven't mentioned your success, the fact that you are still clean. That's a hell of an achievement, something you didn't manage over many attempts in the past. I was wondering, why this time?'

I smile. I had guessed this was coming. 'I think I can explain. Lying on that bed at the beginning of January, I had a glimpse of something that no one should ever see: the gates of hell. And they were slowly opening to let me in. I can never go back there again. If I do, I won't survive. It was terrifying, as though the darkness that had been growing within me for years had lured me there in a final attempt at destruction. It was only in those last few moments that I found the strength to fight back in a way I never had before. Now I understand the reason. My children. If I gave in, I would never see them again. I couldn't let that happen. I know this is going to sound daft, and you'll say it was the toxins and the medication playing havoc with my mind. Perhaps you're right. Perhaps not. It doesn't matter. I know what I saw. Shining through that darkness were Karissa and Ricky, calling me back. That's what saved me and continues to keep me strong now.'

The period between emerging from my detox hell and beginning the regular visits to Raj lasted around three weeks and I spent much of it sitting on my own in my living room. Initially, time dragged. I found it difficult to concentrate. My mind was wandering when I remembered something I had seen on television years before. It was a phone-in on *This Morning*.

A bloke had called in with the same addiction to painkillers as I had. It was ruining his life, he said. He had no motivation to do anything. The medical expert in the studio asked the caller how many pills he was taking. When he replied that he was on 16 at a time, several hits a day, I thought, lucky bastard, who's his doctor? The expert then went on to offer good advice about going to a GP and how there were different pharmaceutical options available to help break the hold the pills could exert. Then Richard Madeley piped up: 'You need to take this one day at a time. If you can't do that, one hour at a time, or one minute at a time.'

That was what I remembered sitting alone in my living room in January 2005. It became my mantra. I used to divide those difficult first few days into quarters: early morning, midday, afternoon, evening. I found it helped me get through, one quarter at a time. Otherwise, each day stretched out ahead of me, long and demoralising.

Very slowly, I was able to start focusing on believing I could be better. I'd been there before, but each time my willpower had let me down. In all those years of abuse and recrimination, however, I had never stood outside those gates and heard the creak of hinges as the doors slowly opened. I couldn't face that again. I wouldn't lose Karissa and Ricky.

I realised I had to take drastic action to change my life if I was to avoid the fate I had glimpsed. If I failed, I might as well be dead. In the past, when I had slipped back into the arms of pills and alcohol, it was because life had never been enough for me, leaving me dissatisfied and disappointed. Willpower alone was never sufficient. I required something real and positive to latch on to. It truly was 'do or die'.

Setting up my own business became my focus and I spent every waking hour thinking about it, planning my future. As I dragged myself out of the horrors of detoxing, before I fully re-entered the real world, I went through a honeymoon period, with no outside pressures and a mind that was beginning to think clearly. Previously, I had wasted such moments on scheming to get hold of tablets and booze. I hadn't wanted to be clean; pills made me feel too good. I had accepted, even hoped, that they would be with me for life.

This time was different. I had new priorities. All my mental energy was directed towards the business and, as each day passed and ideas first trickled and then flooded in, I began to experience something new, a natural high, a buzz produced through healthy thinking. It was incredible.

I felt there was a candle burning within me. It had been there when I was a little girl looking forward to the future, but the darkness had all but extinguished it. Now it was alight once again. It spluttered faintly when I began to reconnect with my brain, it glowed dimly as I envisaged the business, and with every thrilling, exciting, creative idea it grew brighter and stronger, extinguishing the darkness until it no longer infected me. Failure ceased to be an option.

The idea of setting up a cleaning business had been growing steadily in me for some time, despite the lack of nourishment it had received over the past months thanks to my drinking and pill-popping. The original seed had been planted by Ricky, who, on returning from his father's one evening, had mentioned that Dave had been talking about his sister and how successful she had been with her cleaning firm. 'She employs people and has bought a holiday home,' Ricky told me, clearly impressed. Ever competitive, I thought, if she can do it, so can I. The only trouble was I didn't do anything much about it. I couldn't muster the energy or enthusiasm back then.

That was the past.

The first thing I did was put pen to paper, drawing up a sales letter to send out to local businesses. It was a tangible beginning and massively exciting. My heart was thumping, adrenalin coursing through my body. Sleep in this period was fitful at best, an hour here and there as my body attempted to recover from the years of substance abuse and overcome my irregular sleep patterns. Previously, this would have distressed me, sitting alone at odd hours, dissatisfied. Now I had a mission: to refine my letter. I wanted it to be perfect. This was my moment, at last.

The Yellow Pages played a part in my life once again. Where previously it had been the pharmacies section that had become worn out and tattered, now I pored over it searching for full-page ads for companies, copying the most effective words and phrases into my letter. When it was finally completed to my satisfaction, I knew it was good. I had achieved something, but it was only the start.

I decided to call my business Spring Falls Cleaning Services. The inspiration came indirectly from my visits to Blackberry Hill. As the momentum grew, I became receptive to new ideas, open to anything that might bring success. I was sitting in the waiting room before an appointment with Raj, shuffling through the reading material scattered across a table. Amongst the copies of *The Big Issue* and *Venue*, there was a gardening magazine and, flicking through it, I came across a photograph of a gorgeous waterfall. It had an immediate impact and I tore it out. I had my name.

Setting up the business consumed me. There was a lot to do and I was desperate to move things along faster than was perhaps practical given my lack of money. I took to going for a walk every day, regardless of the weather, to clear my head and help me think straight. I had two routes: in the nearby woods and down by the Severn Estuary. Both were beautiful settings and it was an incredibly productive activity. I would take a pen and pad of paper and write down ideas. I began to see the world in a new way. Colours were brighter, sounds sharper. My senses were returning and I embraced them all. I rediscovered the taste of tea and the smell of flowers. I became a different person and began to enjoy life and the delights it offered, big and small. I used to feed the squirrels in the woods, hiding piles of peanuts in special places. When I returned the following day to discover they were gone, I was thrilled.

It was an exhilarating period in my life. My walks laid the foundations of the business, producing countless plans for how it could grow. Coming across a holly bush sparked the idea that I could offer local businesses a 'Christmas sparkle clean' while the offices were closed for the holidays, including a spray of fresh flowers in the reception area to welcome back the staff and help with the post-festive blues. I realised it might not be particularly cost-effective as a one-off, but it would be a great way to get my foot in the door.

That idea proved to be very successful, but not everything took off. On one of my walks along the Severn, I came across a used needle and I thought about offering the council a clean-up service, for the beach and local parks. I wrote to them and was informed that a licence was required to dispose of needles. That was a dead end, as I didn't have the necessary specialist equipment, but it didn't bother me. I was learning all the time. That was what mattered.

What address to put on my letter? I realised that a normal home address wouldn't look very businesslike. I had to come up with something that didn't give the impression that the letter had been sent from a domestic residence. I decided on 'Spring House, Patchway, Bristol' and explained to my postman that anything with that address was to come to me.

The next stage was to begin generating business, which required having my letter printed as a professional leaflet – at no cost to me.

By then, I had been forced to sign on, which I hated. I wanted to fend for myself. Out in the woods, I devised a scheme that would, I hoped, benefit everyone. I made an appointment at what was called the Jobcentre Plus and laid out my idea. 'I want to be self-employed, not dependent on handouts. You want me off your books. If we work together, we can both achieve our aims and save the taxpayer money at the same time. I need sales leaflets printed. If you can cover the cost with a small grant, I will guarantee to stop claiming benefits.'

I made it clear that I wasn't going to be satisfied with anything second-rate. The leaflets had to be glossy, full colour, with the waterfall photograph faded into the background. They went for it and agreed I could print 10,000 leaflets.

I went on to explain that the leaflets would generate leads but that to secure the contracts I had to look the part. Once again, they agreed to my suggestion and arranged for a member of staff to meet me at the mall in Bristol to pay for a business suit I had picked out from Next. It was a black pinstripe costing £150. I looked so professional that I hardly recognised myself.

My leaflets were printed by a local firm, E.G. Brown. This was perhaps the most critical moment in the whole process and I took my time over it, scrutinising the artwork, making adjustments, checking and rechecking a number of drafts before I pressed the button.

The rush when I held that first leaflet in my hand was better than anything I had ever experienced before. My plans were coming together. I was sitting on the doorstep of one of the biggest business parks in Bristol and I knew all about the companies there. Now they were going to find out about me. Karissa was a huge help. I collected businesses' names and addresses from everywhere I could and she created a mail merge on the computer. I was more than happy to target the business parks, delivering my leaflet by hand. Whatever it took, I was prepared to do it. I was also the beneficiary of a well-timed injection of cash that allowed me to purchase a vital piece of equipment, a van.

Towards the end of January, my union representative had contacted me again. I had the right to consult a solicitor at their expense, to discuss a possible claim for unfair dismissal against the nursing home. From the union's perspective, one of their members had been dismissed with no cause. At the meeting, the union's lawyer agreed I had a live claim. I put to one side my dubious activities as a home help and focused on the fact that I had been sacked with no proof of wrong-doing or guilt.

I took up residence in the central library in Bristol, searching through every edition of the *Evening Post* newspaper from the time of my suspension for any admin job advertised at the nursing home. There were enough to give me the necessary ammunition. I accepted the company's offer to settle with a lump sum.

On one of my mailing expeditions, I spotted some Portakabins that had been erected on a nearby building site. They might need some help, I thought. I spoke to the site manager and asked who was responsible for the cleaning. It was one of the labourers and it was clear he wasn't doing a very good job. The manager's cabin office was filthy. Heavy work boots had trailed thick, dark mud everywhere, the bins were overflowing and used mugs decorated most surfaces.

'I live locally,' I told him. 'Would you give me the opportunity to quote for the work?' He agreed and said that if I could keep the price down the job was mine. There was no way I was going to let this opportunity slip by. The name of the company working on the site was McAlpine Construction. It didn't matter that this was only short term. Having such a prestigious firm as my client could make all the difference. I was taken on. All I needed now was to land my first full-blown contract.

We had stuffed hundreds of envelopes and delivered

perhaps a thousand leaflets. The kids knew not to answer the house phone, as that was my business number. All I could do was wait.

The phone rang. 'Good afternoon, Spring Falls Cleaning Services. Laura Walsh speaking. How may I help you?'

It was the office manager for a firm in Avonmouth called Qualitext. She had received one of my leaflets and wanted a quote.

'Certainly, when would it be convenient for me to come round?'

Shit! This is it. The real thing.

I knew what I had to do. I had been phoning round various cleaning firms over the past few weeks, making out I was a large company looking for a quote on cleaning services. From those that came in, the average charge was £12.50 per hour and the style of the documentation gave me a good idea of what I had to produce myself. I was as ready as I would ever be. If I had to blag it at any stage, I would. I wasn't exactly a stranger to making things up. My motto became 'fake it till I make it' and it stood me in good stead.

I arrived half an hour early but didn't go into the building until the agreed time. I wanted to be punctual, not desperate. The woman I had spoken to showed me around the office. I took notes and asked questions. She indicated that she thought it would require three days per week. 'To be honest,' I said, 'I think you only need two.' I deliberately undersold myself, hoping to come across as fair and open. She explained that she was seeing three different companies and would be in touch in due course. At home, I typed up a formal quote, priced it up and sent it off.

A few days later, on my return from my morning walk, the answering machine was blinking. 'Good morning, Miss Walsh. This is Margaret from Qualitext. Many thanks for coming in to see me. I have now received all three quotes for the cleaning services contract. I have to tell you that you were not the cheapest. However, I liked you and thought you were very professional. The job is yours. Please ring me back to make arrangements.'

I stared at the machine. After everything I had been through, after the misery I had inflicted on others, after all my mistakes, I had finally achieved something on my own. I was a businesswoman running my own company.

Karissa and Ricky arrived home. I called them into the living room. 'There's a phone message you should listen to.' Ricky pressed the button. They listened in silence.

When it was over, they turned to look at me and smiled, then said the one thing I had wanted to hear them both say from the day they were born but had never earned: 'We're proud of you, Mum.'

Epilogue
Today

Karissa and Ricky saved me. They held me when I was weak and I will forever be in their debt. And it was my business that offered a road towards salvation from my addictions. With each new cleaning contract I secured, my need for excitement and a sense of worth was nourished. I believe everyone needs goals in life, big or small, and with achievement comes a sense of empowerment, which in my case provided the strength to resist the hypnotic call of pills and booze that had dominated my life for so long.

Prior to establishing Spring Falls, all previous goals I had set myself – Bridge View, challenging the solicitor, employment tribunals – were not truly mine; they were attempts to claim something that wasn't real. You cannot hold a fantasy, but you can hold a truth when it is of your own making.

That initial sense of excitement that comes with embarking on a new adventure cannot last for ever and when it eventually dispersed I was left with a sense of loss. In the past, that would have led down only one path, but creating and running my business gave me the courage and confidence to close off that dark route once and for all. Today, I'm in a far better place in my life than I have ever been before – happy, fulfilled and contented. There are many reasons for that.

I have not had a drink since January 2005. As for the painkillers, that is a blight that I can never totally banish. The secret is to accept that fact and take action. It is six years since I last polluted my system with codeine but I am still on a regular prescription of Subutex, which provides me with the power of control. Previously, that rested with the drug.

I no longer run the business from home. I continue to live in Spring House, but I now have office premises and a staff of 63. The Qualitext contract proved to me, and to many doubting onlookers, that I could succeed. Since then, with the invaluable help of Karissa and friends old and new, my business has gone from strength to strength and now has a turnover of £1 million. On the surface, that may appear a long way from cleaning Portakabins on a building site, but in reality it is not. It is the same business with the same aim – to provide a quality, reliable service at the right price.

We have changed name since those early days. As we grew, it became clear that I would have to register as a limited company. At the same time, I had been considering undergoing a rebranding exercise. Spring Falls had been perfect when I'd first set out, reflecting how I felt, but it was not the future. I had to establish a new, sharper identity. I was discussing various possibilities when Ricky mentioned that he had noticed a van at his place of work with the name Advanced Hygiene Services on it. 'It's brilliant,' he said. I agreed. In particular, I liked the word 'Advanced'. It's at the beginning of the alphabet and it's modern and high tech. It seems to declare, 'We have all the latest equipment.'

I considered Advanced Hygiene and Cleaning Ltd but decided it was too long. I tried Advanced Cleaning, but there were other companies registered under that name. I finally settled on Advanced Cleaning UK Ltd. We haven't looked back.

It hasn't always been an easy journey. It has taken time and patience, with numerous downs as well as ups, but, with the support of many people, we are now a thriving business with more than 50 clients. There is no room for complacency, though. I remain hungry for more success. Along the way, there has been much fun, moments of sadness and some hard and difficult times, but those are stories for another day.

It is perhaps sufficient here to state that I never doubted we would succeed and I am proud we have, reinforcing my belief that with hard work and perseverance anyone can achieve what they want.

There were many times in my life when I thought I would never be able to write the following four words: I am a grandmother. To think I almost let such incredible joy slip away from me. If it had been possible to look into the future and see the wonder that grandchildren bring, I am certain I would never have jeopardised that through reckless self-destruction. But second sight is beyond our capabilities. What we are blessed with is the capacity to envisage what might be – that is the power of hope, the emotion that in many ways defines my life.

Both Karissa and Ricky are healthy, happy and prospering with their partners. Karissa works with me and Ricky is in the building trade. Between them, they have three children. Karissa has Evie, and one on the way, and Ricky has Olivia and baby Alicia. We spend a lot of time together. After so many years of turmoil and distress, we appreciate the moments we have and the memories they create.

As I began to heal myself, I also wished to mend the rifts that had ripped through my life. After years of estrangement, Mum, Dawn and I are building back the bridges we tore down. I know I caused them a lot of hurt in the past, I acknowledge that, but that woman was not truly me. I became upset by their inability to see that I was not myself, that what I said and how I acted did not come from the heart. Those were dreadful years and we all reacted defensively. It is a source of great happiness that we are now putting all that behind us.

The years since I looked on those gates of hell have also brought sorrow. My father died in 2010 and I miss him still. For all that happened between us, he never stopped being Daddy who built my doll's house. I hope with all my heart he is at peace now.

Today

I will always need focus in my life to drive me forward. That became clear as I was writing this book. Whether it was becoming pregnant, creating the perfect family or living in a dream home, I realise now that I jumped from one all-consuming desire to the next. That has not changed. When the business lost the shine of being new and became, well, a business, I moved on to a new obsession, the repercussions of which opened this book. My constant chasing of perfection became focused on my appearance.

I can pinpoint the moment when a vague thought became a burning necessity. It was 2006 and I was in a mall in Bristol, buying a mobile phone. I was sitting at the desk filling out the numerous forms when I heard a wolf whistle behind me. My hair was long and blonde back then and must have caught some young lad's eye. I turned round to see who it was and as I did I heard a sharp intake of breath. 'Eugh!' Yeah, I know, I thought, I don't need you to tell me. My hair promised one thing, but my ravaged face told a very different story. I might have felt young inside, but I looked like a haggard 60 year old. No amount of new business suits was going to change that.

Financially, it was impossible to contemplate any repair work at that stage, but the desire to never again feel as I did in that phone shop did not leave me. A number of months passed before I'd saved enough to undertake my first procedure: a thread lift, which fell short of a full facelift but was more affordable. The intention was to make me look younger and fresher, but I wasn't satisfied with the result. I had expected a miracle, the years of abuse stripped away for ever. All I saw was virtually the same reflection staring back at me.

Radical steps were required, and over the following two and a half years I embarked on a series of what I believed would be transformational operations. In truth, it was a harrowing experience but one I was unable to resist. First, the string that had been implanted during the thread lift worked itself loose and eventually came out, causing me considerable distress. That led to a determination to undergo a full face-and brow-lift, the results of which did not disappoint. But it still wasn't enough; I was addicted. Filler for my lips proved unsuccessful. The results of the tummy tuck were excellent, but the attempts to make my eyes more almond-shaped required multiple surgical procedures. Finally, I took what I promised myself would be the last step: cheek implants. This was towards the end of 2009. By the following spring, I was watching that blood spurt onto my bathroom mirror, before making frantic phone calls to the clinic demanding emergency action to save my face.

Am I happy with how I look now? Yes. Will I ever be totally satisfied? It is not in my nature, no matter how hard I wish it was.

Alan and Dave are still very much part of my life. Alan kept the promise he made in 1999 and has continued to look out for me and has offered much support in the intervening years. Dave and I will never be close again – there has been too much said, too much damage inflicted, for either of us to be able to put the past completely behind us – but he continues to play an active and positive role in Karissa and Ricky's lives. He has been a father to them and for that I am grateful.

A brief, intense but ultimately doomed love affair two years ago acted as the catalyst for me to undertake another important step on my road towards recovery. The romance lasted only three months and, as is common, the first flush was incredibly exciting. I threw myself wholeheartedly into this new passion and, I now realise, it consumed me as so much had before. When it ended, I was devastated, but equally I could sense something was not right. I shouldn't have clung on to the relationship in the manner I did, and I began an attempt to understand myself and my need always to have a major event going on in my life. As I began to assess my failed relationship, the realisation struck me that not everything in my personality was in the right place. Perhaps I was lacking a key ingredient.

Perhaps I still had not dealt with my past sufficiently. I needed to find out.

There were various stop-off points on this journey and I certainly have not reached the destination, but with every discovery comes a degree of understanding that further strengthens my defences. I will never be fully cured, but, provided I continue to move forward, I become more resilient and the risk of regression recedes further into the distance.

Immediately following the break-up, I embraced Emotional Freedom Technique, popularised by Paul McKenna, which looks to dispel the negative energy that may be blocking your growth as a person. It helped mend my broken heart and I still use it today when pressures build and release is necessary.

Traditional counselling has never worked for me. With Raj, I made a connection from which developed a strong rapport, allowing me to open up about my dreams for the future. There is no doubt that those sessions provided invaluable support when I needed it most, but subsequent therapy has failed to strike a chord. However, when I discovered a counsellor who also specialised in EFT, the benefits were immediate and are ongoing. For a brief period, I combined this approach with a technique known as Matrix Reimprinting, which helps you draw the poison out of negative memories. Together, they provided the required nudge towards facing up to my suppressed demons and indirectly led me towards writing this book.

Confronting your mistakes is hard, but when I began to understand the negative power the past held over me, I decided I had to commit my memories to paper. It proved extremely cathartic. I no longer feel I have to hide from my previous self, and with that realisation she has ceased to restrict my development as a person.

Day-to-day strength is vital and I have discovered two sources that provide immense comfort: lavender and crystals. I believe strongly in the healing power of lavender. It has become an integral part of my life. I carry a bottle of its essence everywhere and use drops in my bath to help me relax, on my pillow at night to help me sleep and on my wrists when I can feel myself beginning to become tense.

Sitting here now, writing these closing few pages, I can look around my living room at a variety of crystals, the energy from which provides strength, protection and support. It is impossible to explain, but I believe the benefits these crystals provide are tangible. For instance, a common interest in these ancient and beautiful stones has drawn together a close-knit circle of friends on whom I can rely for support and who know I will always be there for them.

Perhaps most significant of all has been my introduction to the Law of Attraction. Annette's eldest daughter, Simone, a dear friend, recommended Rhonda Byrne's book *The Secret*, and from the moment I began to read it I recognised myself on every page. As I emerged from the despair of that final detox, I focused on what I wanted in life – my business – with a strong belief that I could make it happen. I succeeded. I am convinced that everything in my life up to then happened for a reason, to bring me to that point. I was given the opportunity to produce something positive from so much anguish, but only if I wanted it badly enough and was prepared to work for it. Simplistically, that is the Law of Attraction. In many ways, I had been attempting unsuccessfully for years to utilise this energy, but I was never able to commit fully until that moment. The Law of Attraction has subsequently given context to how I live my life. It is far from a cure-all – it makes no claims to be – but, in helping to make sense of the world, it offers enormous benefits, for me, certainly.

I have listed these various therapies and techniques as an illustration of some of the possibilities that exist if someone seeks a new path. I am in no position to state what would suit any individual other than myself. All I can say is that choices exist. Something will work, if you want it to.

Perhaps the most significant realisation that the years of

self-analysis have brought me, since I cleaned myself up and have been able to think with clarity, unencumbered by chemicals and alcohol, has been that the most destructive driving force in my life has been my need to be needed. When I stopped being a wife or a partner, and as my children grew older and relied on me less, I couldn't take it. That was when the worst of my excesses took hold. I was petrified of being alone.

This desperate desire to be someone exceptional, to stand out, also explains why I tried so hard to banish the commonplace. So I fled from the everyday, which was never enough for me, hiding behind schemes and fantasies and, latterly, substance abuse. That can bring only misery, as you are being false to yourself and to those around you.

This compulsion to be different was warped thinking. As my mind cleared, from 2005 onwards, I began to experience and relish the extraordinary joy of normality and stability. I grew comfortable with my real self, as opposed to the facade I'd tried to erect. I liked being me as I truly am, and flowing from that I grew to appreciate the world around me, where, of course, I am needed – still, indeed forever, as a mother, and as a friend, an employer and, more recently, as one half of a loving partnership. I am needed for the true value I bring to the world, as everyone is in their own sphere. That realisation brought fulfilment and peace, and continues to do so every day.

A large part of the contentment I now feel is thanks to Nathan. Following the crushing disappointment of my previous relationship, I came to believe that I would never find happiness with another person. I did not think I would be open to it, but good has now come out of bad. Nathan and I met a few months ago and I believe we will be together for the rest of our days. We are equal partners who respect each other, love each other and like each other. He makes me laugh and smile. He makes me feel worthwhile and needed – for all the right reasons. I wake up every morning happy to know he is in my life. Thank you, Nathan.

Ashamed

I did not set out to write this book in order to make amends. That should be undertaken in private, not in a public forum. I hope I have taken steps in that respect, but it is a process that will never have a definitive conclusion. Nor am I asking for forgiveness. Others can bestow that if they wish. And I hope these pages are not overflowing with remorse. That was never my intention. I have tried to understand my past, but I know I cannot change it. All I can do is accept responsibility for my actions and try to demonstrate the positive effect that doing so has had, in steering me towards creating a better future for myself and for those I love and care about. Anyone can achieve the same, and if one person attempts to after reading this it will all have been worth it.

I have never written a book before and I have long wondered how I should end it. I have decided to close where I began. The candle I mentioned previously continues to burn and now has a name. My wish is that you too may find a beacon within yourself and keep it alight. The name of my flame? Hope. There is always hope.